THE

PUBLICATIONS

OF THE

Lincoln Record Society

FOUNDED IN THE YEAR

1910

VOLUME 77

ISSN 0267-2634
FOR THE YEAR ENDING 31 AUGUST 1986

THE BOSTON ASSEMBLY MINUTES 1545–1575

Edited by Peter and Jennifer Clark
from a transcript by John Bailey

The Lincoln Record Society

The Boydell Press

First published 1987
for the Lincoln Record Society
by The Boydell Press
an imprint of Boydell & Brewer Ltd
PO Box 9, Woodbridge, Suffolk IP12 3DF
and Wolfeboro, New Hampshire 03894-2069, USA

ISBN 0 901503 50 9

British Library Cataloguing in Publication Data

The Boston Assembly minutes, 1545–1575. —
(The Publications of the Lincoln Record
Society, ISSN 0267-2634; v. 77).
1. Boston (Lincolnshire) — History —
16th century — Sources
I. Clark, Peter, *1944–* II. Clark,
Jennifer III. Bailey, John IV. Lincoln
Record Society V. Series
942.5′37 DA690.B68

ISBN 0 901503 50 9

Library of Congress Cataloging-in-Publication Data

Corporation of Boston (Lincolnshire)
The Boston Assembly minutes, 1545–1575.

(The Publications of the Lincoln Record Society,
ISSN 0267-2634; v. 77)
Includes index.
1. Boston (Lincolnshire)—History—Sources.
2. Great Britain—History—Elizabeth, 1558–1603—
Sources. I. Clark, Peter, 1944– . II. Clark,
Jennifer. III. Bailey, John F. IV. Title. V. Series.
DA670.L69R5 vol. 77 [DA690.B68] 942.5′3705 87-6415
ISBN 0-901503-50-9

This volume has been printed with the help of gifts
from the late Mrs Dawson and the Lincolnshire County Council

Printed in Great Britain by Short Run Press Ltd, Exeter

CONTENTS

Preface

This volume is the product of a division of labour and a degree of co-operation which would have astonished (but one hopes pleased) Tudor Bostonians. The original transcription of the first Boston Assembly Book 1545–1607 was the work of the late Mr John Bailey and a team of local history students under the initial supervision of Dr (now Prof.) Alan Rogers. Part of this research was generously supported by the Leverhulme Trust and further work was undertaken with the considerable assistance of the History of Boston Project and Boston District Council. For this volume Dr Dorothy Owen undertook the task of checking the transcript, as well as providing much needed editorial advice. Mrs Gillian Austen of Leicester University with great patience produced the final typescript. Grants towards the cost of publication were made by Mrs Dawson and the Lincolnshire County Council.

We are indebted to all these people for their help. Finally, we must acknowledge the kind permission of Boston District Council in allowing this calendar of the Assembly minutes to be published.

Introduction

During Elizabeth's reign William Camden described Boston as "a famous town standing on both sides of the river Witham, which has over it a wooden bridge of a great height, and well frequented by the means of the commodious haven unto it . . ."[1] Boston's golden age in the thirteenth and fourteenth centuries as one of the country's leading ports, especially for the export of English wool,[2] had vanished, however, and by the 16th century it was increasingly overshadowed by other east coast ports such as Hull, King's Lynn and Yarmouth. With a population of perhaps 2,000 in the 1560s it now belonged to the ranks, several hundred strong, of England's smaller towns. Yet the town received a significant boost to its fortunes with Henry VIII's grant of a charter of incorporation in 1545. In the following years, as we shall see, Boston's leaders struggled to put the corporation on its feet and to cope with the difficult economic, social and political problems which the town, like many other provincial centres, had to face during the Tudor era.[3]

Regrettably Boston is not well served with historical documentation for the sixteenth century. Apart from the Assembly minutes, the corporation records are meagre.[4] Nor are there substantial collections of material on the town elsewhere. Because of the relative isolation of the community on the edge of the Wash, Boston's inhabitants do not seem to have been active litigants at the Westminster courts and we lack the abundance of central government records which we sometimes find for other towns and which can be so revealing about urban development. Thus the first Assembly minute book which covers the period from June 1545 to May 1607 and which is calendared in part in this volume is an important source for Boston's history in the period after incorporation.

As Camden said, the town straddled the Witham, but the largest part of the settlement was on the east side of the river, near the market place. Boston's

1 W. Camden, *Britain* (London, 1610 ed.), p. 532.

2 S. Rigby, "Boston and Grimsby in the Middle Ages" (paper to the Urban History Conference, Liverpool, 1980); W. I. Haward, "The Trade of Boston in the Fifteenth Century", *Associated Architect. Soc. Reports and Papers*, XLI (1932–3), 169–75.

3 For a general survey of urban problems in the period see P. Clark and P. Slack, *English Towns in Transition, 1500–1700* (London, 1976).

4 For the borough records see the list of "The Records of the Borough of Boston", Lincolnshire Archives Office, 1964.

population, like that of most English towns, grew in the late sixteenth century from 471 households (about 2,000 people) in 1563 to 1,500 communicants (about 2,200 inhabitants) in 1603.[5] The increase was not great but it occurred despite the fact that in most decades there was a large excess of burials over baptisms, particularly during the 1580s.[6] The damp marshy terrain almost certainly contributed to high mortality; plague was another killer. Though the Assembly minutes are silent about the earlier period, they suggest that the town suffered a prolonged and devastating outbreak of plague lasting from March 1586 until the summer of 1588.[7] Mortality may have been further increased in 1586–7 by "the greate dearthe and harde yere" resulting from harvest failure.[8] With persistent natural population deficits, most of the town's growth in the late sixteenth century stemmed from immigration. As elsewhere, there was a growing problem from the late sixteenth century of lower class, subsistence migration. In 1582 and 1590 the Assembly issued orders against the lodging of poor outsiders.[9] Respectable newcomers were rather more welcome, though they had to pay increasingly heavy freedom fines to trade in the town.[10] The important late medieval community of overseas, mainly Hanseatic, merchants had disappeared by this time, but one finds references in the Assembly minutes to a scattering of foreigners in Boston, including Scotsmen. In 1569 two members of the council were dispatched to Norwich to view its Walloon community. The aim was to get some of the leaders to move to Boston to provide work for a number of refugees who had lately arrived there.[11] Four years later the corporation obtained a licence to permit forty families from the Low Countries to settle in the town, but it is unlikely there was a major influx of aliens.[12]

One of the major preoccupations of the corporation in this period was with the haven, the hub of the town's economy. In common with other east coast ports such as Grimsby and Yarmouth,[13] Boston's haven suffered from a serious problem of silting, which was exacerbated by the spread of fen drainage schemes in the area. Precisely how acute the situation was at Boston in the sixteenth century is uncertain. The town leaders complained repeatedly about the decay of the haven, but an official survey in 1565 indicated that it was in

[5] G. A. Hodgett, *Tudor Lincolnshire* (Lincoln, 1975), p. 192; C. W. Foster, ed., *The State of the Church in the Reigns of Elizabeth and James I:* I (Lincoln Record Soc., XXIII, 1926), 313.

[6] P. Thompson, *The History and Antiquities of Boston* (Boston, 1856), p. 105.

[7] Boston, Assembly Book 1545–1607, fol. 233r, 258v.

[8] Ibid., fol. 247v.

[9] Ibid., fol. 203v, 271r.

[10] See entries 548, 632, 688 *et passim.*

[11] See entries 545, 559.

[12] *Calendar of Patent Rolls* (hereafter *CPR*), 1572–5, p. 91.

[13] For Grimsby see E. Gillett, *A History of Grimsby* (London, 1970), p. 120; for Yarmouth, A. R. Michell, "The Port and Town of Great Yarmouth . . . 1550–1714" (unpublished Ph.D. thesis, Cambridge University, 1978), p. 4 *et seq.*

reasonable condition.[14] About this time the town had four official quays, and the Assembly minutes show the corporation was busy keeping clear the main channels to them and repairing the staithes.[15] In the 1570s Boston obtained from the Crown lucrative export licenses for grain with the avowed aim of using the profits to finance the repair of the haven, but how much was spent is not clear.[16]

The deterioration of the haven was not the only difficulty which confronted the port. Shipping was sporadically threatened by marauding pirates. In 1575 the town took into custody several offenders.[17] There were disputes over maritime jurisdiction with the Lord High Admiral, which were not resolved by the grant of certain admiralty privileges to the town in 1573.[18] Even more serious, Boston, five miles from the sea, seems to have suffered from a drift of traffic to minor creeks and upriver ports. By the 1570s small boats with Yorkshire coal and Humber turves were bypassing Boston and unloading at Fosdyke and Fleet.[19]

In comparison to earlier periods the port's importance was sadly diminished. This was particularly evident in overseas trade. The 1565 survey remarked on the recent loss of trade with Flanders and the absence of foreign merchants. Those merchants of the staple still using the port "live in the country and not in the town" and there were "few merchants inhabiting the port". Much of the port's trade was carried on by Lynn merchants. Boston had only eight ships of its own, one of 100 tons, but most under 30 tons; its fleet was no bigger at the start of the seventeenth century. To supplement declining wool exports there was increased shipment of cloth and grain. The corn trade was boosted to some extent by the grant of royal export licenses in the 1570s, but many of these shipments went from Hull and Lynn rather than Boston. As for imports, wine seems to have been the only significant foreign commodity landed.[20]

Like other small ports, however, Boston was able to exploit the vigorous growth of the coasting trade during the sixteenth century. It became a centre for coal imports from Yorkshire and Northumberland, supplying fuel to many of the Lincolnshire towns. In the late 1570s up to forty ships a year were said to have landed coal at the port.[21] As the Assembly minutes make clear, Boston

[14] *Historical Manuscripts Commission* (hereafter *HMC*), Salisbury MSS., II, 315; see entry 95; R. W. K. Hinton, ed., *The Port Books of Boston 1601–40* (Lincoln Record Soc., L, 1956), p. xxxvii; Public Record Office (hereafter PRO), E 178/1273.

[15] Hinton, op. cit., xxvii; see entries 322, 420, 590.

[16] *HMC*, Salisbury MSS., II, 51–2, 315.

[17] See entries 880, 884; see also *Acts of the Privy Council* (hereafter *APC*), 1542–7, p. 535; 1571–5, p. 374; 1577–8, p. 141.

[18] See entry 884; *CPR*, 1573–5, pp. 84–5.

[19] PRO, E 134/22 & 23 Eliz./M 14; Assembly Book, fol. 118v.

[20] PRO, E 178/1273; N. J. Williams, "The Maritime Trade of the East Anglian Ports" (unpublished D.Phil. thesis, Oxford University, 1952), p. 69; Hinton, op. cit., p. xxxv; Hodgett, op. cit., p. 88; for the wine trade in the seventeenth century: *HMC*, Pepys MSS., p. 190.

[21] PRO, E 134/22 & 23 Eliz./M 14.

also retained a share in the fish trade, particularly herring.[22] But here the town's role may have been under pressure from the rise of Yarmouth as the great European fishmarket. In response Boston tried in 1573 to bring in migrants from the Low Countries to set up a herring-curing industry on the Dutch model.[23] Another trade in which the port participated was salt, imported at this time from Scotland.[24] However, one has the impression that Boston failed to maximise its opportunities as an entrepot in the coasting trade. It never became the principal distribution point in the East Midlands for the growing volume of luxury and semi-luxury goods being shipped to the provinces from London in the late sixteenth century.[25] In 1595 the value of the customs at Boston was less than half that of Lynn and was the lowest of all the east coast ports.[26]

Boston had three fairs—the ancient mart at St Andrew's tide and two more, on St George's day and St James' day—granted by Henry VIII's charter. In addition there were markets on Wednesday and Saturday.[27] The Assembly minutes indicate a considerable expansion of market trading in Elizabeth's reign. A series of orders were passed regulating the running of the fairs and markets. In 1568 a market was erected at the Cornhill. In 1573 traders coming to the mart were directed to sell livestock in Bargate, general merchandise along Barbridge street as far as the common staithe, and fish at the gate. In 1576 strict controls were imposed on shops and stalls at the mart.[28] As in other towns, the expansion of trade led to the movement of business away from the formal open market and fair into private houses. In addition the corporation had to contend with an increasing number of non-freemen selling goods in the town, competing with local men.[29]

Turning from trade to industry, the Assembly minutes are not very informative. Five craft gilds were established or recognised in Elizabeth's reign: the tailors; bakers and brewers; glovers; cordwainers; and smiths.[30] In most cases, however, little is known about their activities and it is probable that they catered largely for local demand. Rather more is known about brewing, generally one of the more dynamic industries of the period as a result of a growing consumer taste for new, cheaper, stronger beer instead of the old-style ale. In the 1560s one of the leading aldermen, Thomas Sowthen, was engaged in brewing and one might have expected a buoyant trade with thirsty

[22] See entries 94, 132, 151, 428.
[23] Michell, op. cit., p. 129 *et seq.*; *CPR*, 1572–5, p. 91.
[24] *HMC*, Salisbury MSS, IV, 317; Hinton, op. cit., p. ix.
[25] For the importance of Lynn see Williams, op. cit., p. 159 *et seq.*
[26] *HMC*, Salisbury MSS, V, 393.
[27] Thompson, op. cit., p. 344 *et seq.*
[28] See entries 484, 807, 812, 930.
[29] See entries 132, 238; Assembly Book, fol. 266v, 333v.
[30] See entries: 63 (tailors); 560 (bakers and brewers); 949 (glovers); 163 (cordwainers); Assembly Book, fol. 197v (smiths).

seamen swelling local demand.[31] But Boston brewers faced fierce competition from "country" producers, with beer and ale coming from Lincoln, Lynn and elsewhere. Attempts by the corporation to exclude this foreign beer were unsuccessful.[32]

The retail victualling trade did better. Indeed it was the most notable of the town's service activities. According to the magistrates' return to the Privy Council, part of a national survey of drinking-houses in 1577, Boston had five inns, one tavern and twenty-seven alehouses. The inns and taverns were larger premises which provided for well-to-do merchants and farmers, offering food, drink and, in the case of inns, accommodation. The alehouses were more primitive affairs, often kept in backrooms and serving the poorer orders. Considerable magisterial energy was expended regulating alehouses.[33] By contrast we learn little about other services, such as the work of attorneys and physicians.

The blurred picture presented by the Assembly minutes makes it difficult to reach a firm conclusion about the overall state of Boston's economy in this period. The magistrates frequently protested about the town's decline and won a sympathetic response from the government. In 1572 the Crown spoke of the inhabitants being greatly impoverished and almost utterly declined, while William Cecil, Lord Burghley, included Boston in a list of decayed towns in 1598.[34] But there are signs that while some sectors were faring badly, others, like coastal traffic or marketing, may have been doing better. Camden observed that some of the inhabitants were involved in grazing, benefiting from the rising profits of farming.[35] Even so, the situation was far from buoyant. In the 1550s and after economic decay may have led to the demolition of buildings in the town, with the corporation having to appeal to the Privy Council to stop it.[36]

With the town's economy failing to expand and the population rising, poverty was a growing social problem. In 1568 members of the corporation agreed to contribute to a fund to set the poor on work. Two years later three aldermen and two councillors, together with the mayor's chaplain, were appointed to make a survey of the poor in the town.[37] Because of the town's control over the parish, the Assembly appointed and supervised the collectors and overseers of the poor established by successive Tudor poor laws; some kind of compulsory levy for poor relief was in operation by the 1570s.[38] In

[31] P. Clark, *The English Alehouse* (1983), p. 96 *et seq*.; PRO, E 134/9 Eliz./E 2.

[32] See entries 699, 792, 889; also Assembly Book, fol. 64r.

[33] Clark, *English Alehouse*, p. 42; see entries 536, 741–3.

[34] Thompson, op. cit., pp. 69, 70; *Calendar of State Papers Domestic* (hereafter *CSPD*), 1598–1601, p. 2.

[35] Camden, op. cit., p. 532.

[36] See entries 82, 124, 310; *CSPD*, 1547–80, p. 52; *APC*, 1552–4, p. 182.

[37] See entries 469, 655.

[38] See entries 755–6, 819, 713.

addition to parish relief the corporation took other measures to assist the needy. In bad harvest years like 1573 it established a corn-stock for the poor; a coal-stock came later.[39] In 1578 the Church-house was converted into a house of correction, mainly to deal with vagrants and other incorrigible poor.[40] During the following decade the Assembly intervened on numerous occasions to try to assist the plague victims. The dearth years of the 1590s forced a spate of magisterial action. Grain was purchased from Hull to renew the town's corn stock, and there was a fairly elaborate scheme to set poor boys and girls on work.[41] The local needy also obtained relief from a number of charities established by townspeople.[42]

Predictably the Assembly minutes shed most light on the political and administrative operation of the town after incorporation. One can see first of all some of the problems of setting up the new corporate body, establishing a pattern of administrative continuity. Initial meetings of the Assembly were irregular. Even when meetings were held, mayors too often retained the draft minutes and prevented them being recorded.[43] Following the pattern in other towns, the governing body established by Henry VIII's charter was oligarchic. Power was concentrated in the hands of the mayor and aldermen—a bench of twelve—and the common council of eighteen. Members of the common council were chosen by the mayor and aldermen from the body of burgesses or freemen. Entry to the bench was by co-option from the council.[44] Elections to the mayoralty took place every Lady Day with the common council choosing from several aldermen nominated by the bench; some years the council chose a short-list of candidates before electing the mayor.[45] Oligarchic rule was encouraged by the Crown which preferred to deal with small groups of urban leaders. It was also probably determined in part by the relative shortage of wealthy men in the community, men able to bear the growing burdens of office. From the Assembly minutes it is evident that the corporation experienced considerable difficulty in filling its principal civic offices. This was a general urban problem in the period, but it was apparently acute in Boston. Time and again the Assembly had to lean over backwards to retain the services of leading townsmen. In 1555 William Kyd refused to become mayor and offered to pay a fine instead, but by the entreaty of the whole Assembly agreed in the end to serve the following year. When Alderman Sowthen decided to remove to Peterborough in April 1569 the Assembly spent a whole year trying to get him to change his mind. In 1574 when Alderman Awdley's future wife refused to come and live in Boston, the Assembly promised to release him from the obligation of

[39] See entry 789; Assembly Book, fol. 289v.
[40] Assembly Book, fol. 179v, 207r.
[41] Ibid., fol. 233r, 258r, 338v, 339v, 316r.
[42] See entry 497; Assembly Book, fol. 337r.
[43] See entries 16, 50.
[44] M. Weinbaum, *British Borough Charters 1307–1660* (Cambridge, 1943), pp. 69–70.
[45] E.g., entry 871.

holding office if he dwelt there; no doubt they hoped to retain his informal advice.[46] For the recalcitrant the fine for refusing the mayoralty was increased from £20 to £40.[47] In a small town like Boston, newly incorporated, civic office probably lacked the prestige and influence it enjoyed in larger towns with more ancient corporations. There were compensations, however, for the costs of office-holding. Grants of leases, tolls and other favours were bestowed on members of the bench in particular. Alderman Sowthen was allowed to trade in the town as a brewer though he had never been apprenticed to the trade.[48] In 1593 the incoming mayor was promised a loan of £40, a hogshead of wine and three quarters of wheat, in addition to the customary payment, to help him cover the expenses of his mayoral year.[49]

Closed government inevitably spawned political dissension. The Assembly minutes record sporadic outbreaks of division and factionalism within the corporation.[50] In the 1590s a bitter dispute erupted between Alderman Thomas Tharold and other members of the bench.[51] We also hear complaints against civic rulers by ordinary townsmen.[52] But political tension and animosity does not seem to have become as serious at Boston as in some other urban centres, disrupting civic government. One factor may be that civic finances, often in disarray in other towns and a source of bitter strife,[53] were apparently healthy at Boston. Though the account books are missing for this period, one finds little evidence of serious financial difficulty. During the period after incorporation the borough purchased or obtained substantial amounts of property in and out of the town, including the lordship and various religious properties in 1546, the gild or "erection lands" in 1554, and the manor of Roos in the town (purchased from the Earl of Rutland) in 1557. The corporation was still buying property in the 1590s.[54] The Crown's grants of export licenses for corn, which the town sold to merchants and other interested parties, were also profitable, as was the securing of admiralty privileges in 1573. Finally, there was revenue from market tolls, port duties and other miscellaneous rights. Responsibility for the town's revenues usually lay with two bailiffs or chamberlains though the exact arrangements varied over time.

With its extensive property holdings the corporation devoted a sizeable part of its time to the general administration of the town estate—making leases, surveying holdings, ensuring repairs were carried out. Another major

[46] See entries 172, 558, 598, 842–3.
[47] See entries 173, 546.
[48] PRO, E 134/9 Eliza./E 2.
[49] Assembly Book, fol. 295r.
[50] See entries 294, 338, 356, 948.
[51] Assembly Book, fol. 327r, 331r, 350r.
[52] Ibid., fol. 164r–v.
[53] Clark and Slack, op. cit., p. 130 *et seq.*
[54] Thompson, op. cit., pp. 64, 66; see entry 201; Assembly Book, fol. 320v.

administrative concern (already mentioned) was the maintenance of the port—levying dues, ordering the scouring of channels and the maintenance of the quays. When the town bridge fell down in March 1556/7, speedy measures had to be taken for its replacement.[55] Economic matters also preoccupied the magistracy with the assessment of wages, the setting of prices of beer, candles and coals, the regulation of the gilds and markets, and the licensing of alehouses.[56] As in other sixteenth-century towns there were moves to improve the water supply, to cope with the increased population.[57] Following the corporation's purchase of the rectory of Boston in 1546 the Assembly also took an active role in ecclesiastical affairs in the town, appointing ministers, auditing the churchwardens' accounts, repairing the church fabric, using income from the rectory to pay the mayor's annual expenses.[58]

A final major responsibility of the corporation concerned relations with the outside political world, now dominated by the growing power of the Crown and of the landed gentry. Here Boston's leaders showed themselves strikingly successful in furthering the interests of their small town. Despite all the twists and turns of royal policy, Boston managed to extract important political and economic concessions from the Tudor regime. After Henry VIII's charter of incorporation, the town secured the right to elect MPs in 1547, while Mary gave it the extensive erection lands in 1554 to maintain the town grammar school and repair the bridge and port. Under Elizabeth, Boston acquired the admiralty jurisdiction over the port and other privileges.[59] One key to the town's success was its long-standing connection with William Cecil, Lord Burghley, Elizabeth's Lord Treasurer. Keen to consolidate and enlarge his political base in Lincolnshire, Burghley proved an invaluable patron and ally of Boston. As well as helping it obtain the admiralty rights and corn export licenses, he facilitated the admission of a number of Boston merchants to the London Company of Merchant Adventurers in 1576. In later years the magistrates regularly appealed to him for his help in resolving problems with outsiders.[60] Burghley became Recorder of the borough in 1545, while his son Thomas was a beneficiary of the corn licenses.[61] In 1578 the whole corporation went in person to Burghley House, near Stamford, to thank him for his favour, taking with them gifts of oxen, wethers and fowl.[62] The town also cultivated other political patrons, including Edward, Lord Clinton, Earl of Lincoln and Lord High Admiral, and his son Henry. The Clintons had an important estate

[55] See entries 190, 196, 209.
[56] Assembly Book, fol. 64r, 164r; see entries 13, 23, 75, 923.
[57] See entries 498, 517.
[58] See entries 43, 117, 689, 844; Assembly Book, fol. 295r.
[59] S. T. Bindoff, ed., *The House of Commons 1509–58* (London, 1982), I, 133; Thompson, op. cit., pp. 66–7; *CPR*, 1572–75, pp. 84–5, 166.
[60] Thompson, op. cit., 73, 341; Assembly Book, fol. 179v, 201r.
[61] Bindoff, op. cit., p. 133; see entries 896–7, 909, 911.
[62] Assembly Book, fol. 182r.

at nearby Tattershall. The father was elected Steward of the town, and in 1572 was given the right to nominate one of the town's MPs.[63]

Boston's contacts with outside magnates were not universally harmonious, however. In 1552 the town resisted unsuccessfully demands by the Marquis of Northampton for a release of the gild lands (though they recovered them under Mary). Relations with Lord Willoughby proved contentious under Elizabeth and there was also conflict with local landowners like William Hunston and Leonard Craycroft.[64] In the 1580s the town fought hard to muster its troops separately from the county—only to be overruled on this occasion by Burghley. In the last part of Elizabeth's reign Boston joined forces with Hull and Lynn to oppose the depredations of the white salt patentees.[65]

Servicing the multifarious activities of the corporation were a small number of officers, the town clerk, the husband (in charge of the town's works), the serjeants, the beadle, and the porters. Of these the most important by far was the town clerk. George Forster, the first clerk, who played a major role in setting up corporate administration also served as MP from 1553 to 1558, and later became an alderman.[66] Usually they were attorneys with county ties, though George Allen, appointed in 1562, was a Londoner.[67] In 1552 the Assembly ordered that appointments to these offices should be made annually, but the rule was enforced only sporadically and officers frequently served for years at a time, providing much needed continuity.[68]

During the mid-Tudor period the corporation appears to have conformed to the sudden shifts of official religious policy. The surviving Assembly minutes reveal no opposition to the Protestant innovations of Edward VI or to the Catholic restoration under Mary. From the 1560s, however, there are indications that a number of town leaders favoured a stronger commitment to the cause of godly religion. In 1568 the Assembly appointed a town preacher. In later years it agreed to pay for funeral sermons for members of the corporation, public subscriptions were raised for town sermons, and special seating arrangements made for magistrates to hear the preacher in church.[69] There was a growing campaign against moral offenders. In 1574 the Assembly condemned and fined Alderman Christopher Awdley for adultery, using powers granted in the 1573 charter. Later in the reign Boston clashed with the High Commission over its prosecution of such offenders and other innovations, but in general the growing ascendancy of civic Puritanism went unimpeded, aided by the corporation's tight control over the town living, its geographical isolation, lax diocesan control, and the possible favour of

[63] See entries 672, 717, 729.
[64] See entries 67, 69; Assembly Book, fol. 211r; see entries 372, 929.
[65] Assembly Book, fol. 192v; *CSPD*, 1580–90, p. 641; *APC*: 1590, p. 186; 1591, pp. 37–8.
[66] Bindoff, op. cit., p. 133; see entry 41.
[67] See entry 365.
[68] See entry 52.
[69] See entry 474; Assembly Book, fol. 191r, 281v, 343r, 261v, 283v.

Burghley.[70] By the early seventeenth century Boston had become a major Puritan stronghold.[71]

In tune with the growing emphasis on a godly community there was a new stress on learning. The grammar school endowed by Mary's grant of the erection lands expanded under Elizabeth. In 1567 a new school house was erected at a cost of over £195, and an usher or second master was appointed. Thereafter the school has a continuous history.[72] The period also saw traditional plays, processions and rites phased out and their replacement by civic ceremonies associated with the ruling body. In the 1560s the Assembly ordered members of the corporation to attend the mayor in procession on St George's Day and St James' Day when the fairs were opened. From 1575 they escorted the mayor to church after the annual civic election on Lady Day.[73] By then the magistracy was firmly in charge of the town and its public world.

Although a great deal has been written in recent years about the major cities and towns of provincial England in the Tudor and Stuart period, our knowledge of the numerous smaller towns, their social and economic life and political fortunes, remains surprisingly incomplete. Although the Assembly minutes calendared below may lack the high drama and vivid detail to be found in the conciliar records of some larger urban communities, they do provide interesting insights into the governmental processes and problems of the small town. At Boston the overall picture is one of a rather fragile urban existence with a paucity of civic magnates and considerable economic and other difficulties to overcome, but of a corporation seizing every political opportunity to consolidate the town's position, to enable it to recover and flourish again in the future.[74]

[70] See entries 820–1; Assembly Book, fol. 259r, 271v.

[71] For the later history of Puritanism at Boston see H. Hajzyk, "The Church in Lincolnshire c. 1595–1640" (unpublished Ph.D. thesis, Cambridge University, 1980), p. 133 *et passim*.

[72] See entries 435, 488, 466; Thompson, op. cit., p. 284 *et seq*.

[73] See entries 10, 453, 951; Assembly Book, fol. 179v.

[74] For Boston's revival after the Restoration see E. J. Dawson, "Finance and the unreformed boroughs . . . with special reference to the boroughs of Nottingham, York and Boston" (unpublished Ph.D. thesis, Hull University, 1978), p. 3 *et seq*.

Editorial Note

The first 164 folios of the first Assembly Book of Boston have been calendared covering the years 1545–75. It was felt that this would shed interesting light on the early years of the corporation and give a broad indication of the range of material to be found in the Assembly minutes during the 16th century. Entries for the first six meetings (1 June 1545–30 May 1547) appear in transcript. Most other entries have been calendared in modernised form, but important sections of the text are printed in full. Contractions have been expanded. In the calendar personal and place names have been standardised. A summary of orders on folios 56–65r has been omitted, as also have folio headings giving the name of the mayor and/or year.

1 June 1545 Assembly

"THE FIRST daye of June in the xxxvij yere of the reygne of our Sofferaigne lorde Henry the VIII^{te} by the grace of god Kyng of englonde Fraunce and Irelonde, Defendor of the Faythe and of the churche of englonde and also of Irelonde in erthe the supreme Hede NICHOLAS ROBARTSON, esquyre Maior of this Borrowe of Boston, by the Aucthorytie of the Kinges maiesties Charter, Dyd take his corporall othe in the Guyhalde of the said borrowe in the presence of the Recorder, the xij Aldermen and the Inhabitantes of the said borrowe. fol. 1v. 1

THE same day the xij^{te} Aldermen of the said borrowe that is to wytt Nicholas Felde, John Tupholme, John Wendon, John Taverner, William Spynkes, William Kyd, Thomas Sorsbye, Harrye Foxe, William bollys, John Margerye, William Ysott and Harry Hoode, by the auchorytie of the said Charter dyd take ther corporall othes. 2

THE SAME day also Richard Gooddyng gentyllman, was electe and chosen Recorder of this said borrowe and toke his othe before Mr Mayer and his brethern the Aldermen, and he to have for a yerly annuytie or Fee grauntyd to him by patente vj^{li} xiij^{s} iiij^{d} to be payde hym ij tymys in the yere as apperyth by the sayd patente. 3

ALSO the seconde day of the same Monethe, George Forster Was electe and chosen to be Town clarke of this borrowe of Boston, and he to have a yerlye Fee of iij^{li} vj^{s} viii^{d} and took his othe the same tyme in the said guylhalde. 4

The same day was William Wymarke & Nicholas Smythe electe and chosen Seriantes at the Mace of this borrow and Sworne before Master Maior and his brether the Aldermen and to be gatherers of the Tolle, and ether of them to have for ther yerly wagys xxvj^{s} viij^{d} and a lyveraye and Mr Maior to be at the charge of the bordyng every weke of one of them to wate uppon hym at hys table that is to wytt the one Seriante to wayte uppon hym at hys table one weke and the other fol. 2r. 5

Seriant the other weke and so chaung-gyng from weke to weke And uppon the sondays and holly days both the Seriantes to wayte of master Maior at his table.

6 The same day also was Thomas Radforth electe and chosen the Maiors Clarke and Water baylyfe and sworne and he to have for his ffee xl^{s}.

7 And the same day was Thomas Smyth chosen to be the Bedell of this Borrow.

4 February 1545/6 Assembly
Assemble holden the iiij^{te} day of february 1545

8 At this assemble Leonard Bowsher was chosen to be the Maiors clarke in thomas Radforth rowme and had his fredome gyven him frelye and so first toke his othe as a freman and then for his office.

25 March 1546 Assembly
Assemble holden in the guihald the xxvth day of Marche beyng our Ladys Day for the election of the new Maior for the yere followyng

fol. 2v. At the same Assemble it was agrede that the office of the Mairaltie
9 shold go frome one to another as the Kyng Maiestie hadde nomynated them in the charter, excepte ther sholde other cawses reasonable be fownde, And so Mr felde was chosen to be the Maior for the yere folowynge.

11 June 1546 Assembly
fol. 3r. At an assemble holden by Mr Maior, the aldermen and the Commen
10 Councell the xith day of June in the xxxviijth yere of the Reingne of Kyng Henry the viijth yt was determynyde and agrede that the Raymentes shold not goo in processyon for that yere.

11 Also yt ys determyned by the Mayor, Aldermen and commen councell aforsaid that they sholde survaye and vyewe all suche voyde growndys as do belong or perteyne unto the toune and the liberties of the same And so to cawse yt to be inclosede to the commen use and proffite of the toune aforsayd.

12 Also yt ys agreed by the Maior and the Aldermen aforsaid that Leonard Bowsher sholde occupye the office of a seriante, beying the maiors clarke also.

blank fol. 3v.

7 March 1546/7 Assembly

At An Assemble holden by Master Mayor and his bretherne the vijth fol. 4r.
Daye of Marche in the Firste yere of the Reinge of Our Soveraing **13**
Lorde Kyng Edward the VJth yt was condescendyd and agrede that the bruarys of this borroughe of boston shall brwe after 1^{d} the gallon of goodale and doble bere after 1^{d}/ob the gallon And syngle bere at 1^{d} the gallon accordyng to the statute therfore provyded after the pryce of Malte in the markyte and the contreth ale to be solde after 1^{d}/ob the gallon.

30 May 1547 Assembly

At an Assemble holden the xxxth day of Maye by Mr Maior and the Aldermen it was determyned and agrede that the seriantes of this borrough shall reken every weke thone to the other accomptyng trulye of all suche profytes as shalbe gotten bye them, or ether of them by Reason of ther office. **14**

And also yt ys determyned and agreed that bothe the Seriantes shall put in sureties to be bownde to Mr Maior his brethern and ther successors in an hundreth markes sterlyng every of them for the dewe execucyon of ther office. **15**

1548 *marginal note*

John Wendon Maior who allways carryd home with hym the Notes for the assembles in the tyme of hys Mairaltie savyng one pamplete. fol. 4v. **16**

26 May 1548 Assembly

William Brynklay and Richard Wace elected Aldermen. **17**

William Smyth, John Stephenson and John Gooddale elected to the Common Council. **18**

Marshall the town Bailiff to bring a bill for the workmen to the mayor each week to be paid. **19**

Sessors appointed for the tax: Mr Kyd, Mr Sorsbye, Mr Fox, Mr Dobb, William Bryan, John Parrowe, Robert Taylor, Robert Warde, Stephen Clarke, John Maston, Simon Melsonbye, William Pottes. **20**

fol. 5r. *10 August 1549 Assembly*

21 Both the Serjeants to put in sureties for their office.

22 Leonarde Bowshere the Clerk complained that his wages were too low; he is to be allowed one half of the profit of the "strete" [estreats] and the profits of the market court.

23 December 1549 Assembly

23 Agreed that no ship coming to the port of Boston laden with coal, whether a ship belonging to the town or strangers, may "sell upon the water" any coals from the ship at a higher rate than the mayor's price, upon pain of double forfeiture of the excess price; provided that this order "shall not be preiudycyall to any freman within this towne to lande and seller his colys and to sell them at his wyll and plesure after he have so sellerde them or layde them uppe in his yarde".

fol. 5v.

24 Also agreed that "forasmuche as by the Kynges Iniuncyons every towne is commaundyde to pay to the parson or proprietorye for the chargys of the communyon every Sonday, such sumys of Money as to fore was customyd to be bestowyd on hollye brede, from hence forth every Inhabytor within this towne (beyng estemyde worth xl^{s}) shall pay every Sondaye viij^{d} when it shall come to his cource at the recevyng of the communyon accordyng to the said Inyuncyons and to begynne on Sonday nexte after the Date herof wher the said Holly brede lefte".

31 January 1549/50 Assembly

25 Agreed that every inhabitant when he pays 8d to the parson for holy bread, shall also pay an extra penny to the clerk every Sunday for warning him.

26 No freeman to sue another freeman outside the borough or within it (without the Mayor's licence), either over land or any other matter upon pain of 40s.

fol. 6r.

fol. 6v. *blank*

fol. 7r.

4 May 1550 Assembly

27 The Mayor to ride to London on the town's affairs, Simon Melsonbye with him.

28 Mr Felde appointed to oversee the repair of the broken staith.

Mr Nicholas Robartson to be the Mayor's deputy. **29**

"At the same assemble was Redde the names of the Inhabytaunce that was not free of the corporacion. And it is agrede that they shal be callyd before the Maiers Deputy". **30**

Timber to be bought for the town's affairs. **31**

5 June 1550 Assembly

Thomas Wyberde failed to answer for 14s which he owes on the account of the late St George's gild;[1] referred to the next assembly. **32**

The "Bedemen Garth" to be let out. **33**

The Bridge to be viewed and mended. **34**

Christopher Hix and Richard Kirkbye to be allowed to present their accounts the next morning. **35**

The Mayor and his brethren to pay for the common sewers and the Cow Bridge when the charge is known. fol. 7v. **36**

"The same day was broken up the Comission of ye Sewers and ij other wrytts concerning the same". **37**

"When the same commyssion was broken uppe Mr Wendon Mr Kyd Mr Turner, Mr Parrowe and Mr Huntwike toke ther corporall othe, accordyng to the Kynges commyssion of Sewers aforsaid" **38**

The Sergeants at the Mace took their oaths according to the writ directed to the Mayor and the Commissioners of Sewers **39**

Mr Mayor, Mr Robartson, Mr Felde, Mr Wendon, Mr Kyd and other Aldermen to consider what should be done about the whitening of the church, the high quire and St Peter's. **40**

The Serjeants and the Water Bailiff to render their accounts weekly. **41**

[1] St George's gild was one of five incorporated gilds in the town; the others were Corpus Christi, St Mary's, St Peter and Paul, and Trinity. Most of them were dissolved in the 1540s.

16 June 1550 Assembly

fol. 8r. Present: Mr Mayor, Mr Robartson, Mr Felde, Mr Tupholme, Mr
42 Wendon, Mr Kyd, Mr Dobbes, Mr Turner, Mr Ware, Mr Parrowe, Mr Huntwike, Aldermen; William Bryan, Robert Stubbes, Simon Melsonbye, John Mason, Andrew Tompson, John Goodale, William Smyth, John Stevenson, Christopher Hix, Christopher Walker, John Eldrede, Common Council.

43 Goodlake Chapman, Christopher Hix and Thomas Marre, Churchwardens, presented their accounts and were discharged.

44 Christopher Walker, John Goodale and John Eldrede presented their accounts, paid their money and were discharged.

20 June 1550 Assembly

45 Agreed that the dispute between John Felde and John Stubbes over "the shippe ladyng of coles" be determined by the Mayor.

30 September 1550 Assembly

46 "Agreed that no turves shall passe thorowe the brydge to the salt cottes, but to Remayne in the towne frome tyme to tyme and to take ther markyt at which day thes keles (whose names do followe on the other side) were stopped:

Christopher Lane	a kele
William Kammocke and chester	a kele
Redeshawe	kele
Kyme	ij keles
Stavyne & Cade	a kele

fol. 8v. And also other ij keles all then beyng laden."

4 October 1550 Assembly

47 An indenture of covenants for a patent for John Browne sealed in the presence of Mr Mayor, Mr Tupholme, Mr Wendon, Mr Kyd, Mr Turner, Mr Huntwike, Mr Parrowe.

4 March 1550/1 Assembly

48 "There was showed certen articles concernyng the lands late Corpus Christi and nowe to the corporacion for an answere to be made to the Lorde Admyrall".

9 April 1551 Assembly

49 Leases sealed for: Mr Tupholme, Mr Wendon, Mr Kyd, Mr Felde, Leonard Bowshere, Thomas Swyllyngton, Margaret Rede, William Callowe, Thomas Deanes, Mr Dobbes, Jane Shepard, Andrew Kytchyn.

1551 Henry Fox Mayor fol. 9r.

"This man toke home with hym all his pampletes of Assembles and so are lost and not regestrede". **50**

23 May 1552 Assembly

Lease for 13 years to Robert Myckelbarrowe of the house now occupied by Robert Gray. fol. 9v. **51**

All officers including the Mayor's clerk, the Serjeants, Husband, Beadle and Porters to be discharged once a year and reappointed if thought fit; all officers that have any charge to put in sureties. **52**

Thomas Sowthen and Simon Melsonbye were chosen aldermen. **53**

27 May 1552 Assembly

Simon Melsonbye took the oath as alderman. **54**

Agreed that no corn be sold in the market before 8 am between the feast of the Annunciation [25 March] and Michaelmas, or before 9am between Michaelmas and the Annunciation on pain of a fine of 12d per sack on the seller. **55**

No baker or brewer to buy any grain in the market before 11 am; no baker to stay any grain in the market before this time; upon fine of 6d per strike for both offences. **56**

Officers discharged and readmitted: Leonard Bowshere, Clerk; Richard Draycott, Serjeant (upon sureties); Thomas Smyth, Beadle. fol. 10r. **57**

28 May 1552 Assembly

All beer and ale brewers present. The beer brewers ordered not to sell double beer above 2d the gallon, or single beer above 1d the gallon until a new assize is set. **58**

Likewise, the ale brewers not to sell "good ale" above 2d the gallon, or small ale at less than 3 gallons for 1d. **59**

14 June 1552 Assembly

Thomas Sowthen took the oath as Alderman. **60**

John Margery and William Hawkrige were elected to the Common Council. **61**

John Bell, mercer, and John Gawdrye, draper, took their oaths as members of the Common Council. **62**

63 Articles concerning the occupation of tailors were read and deferred to a further meeting.

64 Martin Bradley, merchant, took the oath as a member of the Common Council.

fol. 10v.
65 Mr Wendon's account for town business in London was approved.

18 June 1552 Assembly

66 William Hawkrige, saddler, and John Margery, butcher, took their oaths as members of the Common Council.

21 June 1552 Assembly

67 "At this assemble the letters were oppened sent from the Lorde Marques of Northampton who hath obtayned at the Kynges maiestie handes all the late gilde lands that perteyned to the corporacion of Boston as our ladys, saynt peters, the Trynytie and sant George, to the Maier and burgesses of this burrowgh of Boston requiryng ther Release for the same, and the Maier then callyng all the howse desyred every to sett his hand to the book of pamplettes or remembraunces who wolde consent therto and who wolde not, and so they dyd."

Names of the aldermen that do not consent to the releasing of the lands: Henry Hoode, Mayor (two voices), Mr Wendon, Mr Sorsbye, Mr Turner, Mr Dobbes, Mr Parrowe, Mr Palmer, Mr Sowthen.

Names of the Aldermen that do agree to the release: Mr Felde, Mr Tupholme, Mr Kyd.

fol. 11r. Names of the Common Council that do not consent: Robert Stubbes, Richard Clarke, Stephen Clarke, John Stevenson, John Bell, John Gawdrye, William Smyth, Andrew Tompson, John Eldrede, John Margery, William Hawkrige. Absent: Robert Warde, Christopher Walker, John Mason, Christopher Hix, John Goodale, Martin Bradley, Robert Bryan.

21 June 1552 Assembly "at one of the clocke at afternone"

68 "At the same assemble for dyvers consideracions them movyng (allthough heretofore sundry and most of them hath thought convenyent that they sholde seale no release for all the said gild landes) yet nevertheless (for avoydyng of further daunger) they thynke and do holly agree (that uppon certen condicions) they will make a Release or surrendre that is to say to have this hall and tharrerages with other thynges as may be obteyned".

9 July 1552 Assembly

At this assembly it was agreed that the surrender or release be delivered to the Lord Marquis' surveyors by the mayor for the lands of Our Lady, St Peter, the Trinity and St George, and those present set their hands to the book of Remembrances for the Assemblies: Henry Hoode, Mayor, Nicholas Felde, John Wendon, William Kyd, Thomas Sorsbye, Harry Fox, Edmund Turner, Robert Dobbes, John Parrowe, Lawrence Palmer, Aldermen; John Mason, John Eldrede, Robert Stubbes, Stephen Clarke, John Goodale, Robert Warde, John Gawdrye, John Bell, John Margery, Common Council. **69** fol. 11v.

19 July 1552 Assembly

The oaths of the freemen, and the ordinances for disobeying the payment of forfeitures, assessments and impositions read, because John Mason had refused to pay 6s 8d, part of the 20s fine for his freedom. After discussion it was agreed that Mason should pay the amount at 3s 4d a year. **70**

23 August 1552 Assembly

Deeds sealed for the house sold to John Rowte at Skirbeck Gowt, and a lease to Robert Myckelbarrowe for the house that Gray dwells in. **71**

6 October 1552 Assembly

Agreed that communication be had with Vicar Sandforth[2] for the surrendering of his benefice. Creditors of the goods late William Brynklay's to be warned to bring in their money on 13 October. **72**

Agreed that the late Mayor and Bailiffs present their accounts on 13 October. **73**

The kitchen under the town hall and the chamber over it to be converted to a prison and a dwelling for one of the Serjeants. fol. 12r. **74**

The Mayor to set the price for chandlers: the present rate is 2½d in the lb. **75**

Roger Bentley alias Dowce discharged from his freedom for not paying the fine. Only to be readmitted it he pays the full fine again. **76**

[2] Baron Sandford, vicar 1545–54.

31 October 1552 Assembly

77 "At this Assemble it is agrede that this acte shalbe a sufficient discharge for Henry Hoode now the Maior of and for all maner of goodes as procession garmentes and other thynges solde by hym of late in the guihald as by a byll of the perticulars doth appere whereunto certen of the Aldermen hath subscribed ther names".

78 Also agreed that Mr Mayor and Mr Sowthen shall go to London about the town's affairs.

79 Robert Stubbes was elected an Alderman.

80 John Dove was elected to the Common Council.

81 Lease of the "Bedemens garthyng" granted to Simon Melsonbye for 21 years at 7s a year.

24 November 1552 Assembly

82 "At this Assemble a letter sent from the councell concernyng the non pullyng downe of howses was redde and regestred.

83 A letter from Sir William Almondson read concerning "habrams rayment".

8 December 1552 Assembly

fol. 12v. **84** Christopher Hix discharged as Bailiff and ordered to present his account.

13 December 1552 Assembly

85 The assessment book for the church was read and totalled at £24 1s.

12 December 1552 Assembly

86 In answer to the letter of Mr Hall concerning Mr Naunton's[3] fee it was agreed to offer 40s.

87 The leather forfeited by the tanner, Sir Nicholas Felde, shall be sold to some saddler for the benefit of the hall, and Felde be granted 26s 8d.

88 Roger Bentley alias Dowce submitted and asked for his freedom again. Fine agreed at 26s 8d with 6s 8d paid now and the remainder at 5s a year.

[3] William Naunton of Alderton, Suffolk, former servant of the Duke of Suffolk; MP for Boston in 1547.

9 January 1552/3 Assembly
John Dove took his oath as freeman. **89**

Whereas Dove was nominated one of the Eighteen, he is now discharged of the Common Council and it is agreed that if he is hereafter chosen he shall not hold office above 48 hours. **90**

18 January 1552/3 Assembly: attended by the Mayor, Recorder, Aldermen and Common Council. fol. 13r.
Concerning Mistress Naunton's suit against the town for [her husband's] fee for attending Parliament, Mr Forster was authorised to deal with it, offering 20 nobles or less to her in the meantime. **91**

Mr Forster to obtain a release from the Marquis of Northampton for the town's former arrears, and also get a letter to Mr Hunston for his release of the guildhall. **92**

Vote on whether Mr Fox, late Mayor, should be allowed 24s 8d for "the eatying of venyson" and for making his accounts. Those against: Simon Melsonbye, Thomas Sowthen, Robert Dobbes, Thomas Sorsbye, Mr Kyd, Mr Felde, Henry Hoode, Mayor. Those in favour: John Parrowe, Mr Wendon, Mr Tupholme, Mr Recorder. **93**

24 January 1552/3 Assembly
"At this Assemble the Northfolke & suffoke men came to the hall for the prices of ther wares and the price was then as folowyth **94**

White Heryng full	xj^{li} the	last $xviij^{s}$ $iiij^{d}$ barr
White shotten	ix^{li}	last xv^{s} barr
Redde full	ix^{li}	last ix^{s} cade
Redde shotten	vij^{li}	last vij cade
Sprattes	$xxvj^{s}viii^{d}$	last $ij^{s}viii^{d}$ kympe."

25 January 1552/3 Assembly
Mr Fox's account for his mayoralty was found in arrears of £61 9s 9d. fol. 13v. **95**

"Also at the same assemble ther was a letter redde sent frome Master ogle concernyng the graunt of one of the burgesses romes of the parlyament for Thomas Ogle his sonne, wheruppon it was agrede that Mr Ogle sonne was to younge and not mete for that office". **96**

27 January 1552/3 Assembly
Richard Draper elected to the common council. **97**

98 Writ from the Sheriff of Lincolnshire for choosing two Burgesses for Parliament read. Agreed that Leonard Irby[4] should be one, "not havyng or takyng any fee or wage for the same", and the other choice deferred to the next assembly.

29 January 1552/3 Assembly

99 Agreed that George Forster[5] according to his request should be the other burgess; a letter certifying the burgesses' names was sent to the sheriff.

23 March 1552/3 Assembly

fols. 14–15 *missing*

[?1554] Assembly

fol. 16r. £26 13s 4d owed to Mr Wendon for 226 days service at 3s 4d per
100 day.

101 Present: Lawrence Palmer, Mayor; Mr Tupholme, Mr Wendon, Mr Felde, Mr Fox, Mr Dobbes, Mr Parrowe, Mr Melsonbye, Mr Bryan, Mr Johnson, Aldermen; Stephen Clarke, William Smyth, John Goodale, Christopher Walker, Bartholemew Grantham, John Mason, Christopher Hix, Andrew Tompson, Richard Draper, Common Council.

25 May 1554 Assembly

102 Alyne Lodde, Serjeant, was discharged and paid 6s 8d for his quarter's wage.

103 Thomas Smyth, the Beadle, was discharged and re-admitted to office.

104 Thomas Smyth is to have half of the money due for measuring salt and is to pay the rest to the mayor for the use of the hall.

105 All the porters were discharged and re-admitted to office.

106 Robert Inman and John Dyker were appointed to collect the water tolls and deliver the money at the end of each week to the Mayor, who will pay them for their pains according to the rate; they should have a book made of the toll rates.

[4] Leonard Irby of Sutterton and Boston, clerk of the peace for Lincolnshire; MP 1553, 1554–71.

[5] George Forster, town clerk, and MP 1553–8.

Christopher Hix and Stephen Clarke were chosen to collect the town's rents for the year from last Michaelmas. They are to have the accustomed fees and a rental given them. And so the rents shall be gathered yearly by two of the Common Council appointed by the whole house "that everyone that shalbe of the howse may knowe the Townes lands". fol. 16v. **107**

Present: Lawrence Palmer, Mayor; Mr Kyd, Mr Fox Mr Parrowe, Mr Dobbes, Mr Bryan, Mr Melsonbye, Aldermen; Stephen Clarke, Christopher Hix, Goodlake Chapman, John Eldrede, William Smyth, John Goodale, Richard Draper, John Margery, Christopher Walker, Martin Bradley, Common Council. **108**

1 June 1554 Assembly

John Mason, one of the Common Council, chosen Coroner in the borough. **109**

Richard Wynter appointed one of the Serjeants, on giving sureties. **110**

Present: Lawrence Palmer, Mayor; Mr Tupholme, Mr Wendon, Mr Kyd, Mr Dobbes, Mr Johnson, Mr Bryan, Mr Melsonbye, Aldermen; Stephen Clarke, Goodlake Chapman, John Stevenson, John Eldrede, John Goodale, Christopher Hix, John Mason, William Smyth, Andrew Tompson, John Margery, Common Council. fol. 17r. **111**

2 June 1554 Assembly

Richard Wynter took his oath as Serjeant and received the mace. **112**

2 July 1554 Assembly

The account book of Robert Myckelbarrowe, Bailiff, was added up, and £175 19s 1d found due. Of this he asked to be allowed £13 11s 1d "that is in decay and cannot be gotten", and £111 12s paid to Mr Dobbes; and so he owes £50 16s. **113**

At this assembly Bartholemew Grantham, Richard Draper and Christopher Stamper, Constables, received their book again, which they had delivered to Mr Dobbes, in order that they might collect the oustanding money, except from the twelve aldermen, and complete their accounts. **114**

Present: Lawrence Palmer, Mayor; Mr Wendon, Mr Kyd, Mr Fox, Mr Dobbes, Mr Sowthen, Aldermen; Christopher Hix, William Smyth, Richard Draper, Bartholemew Grantham, Common Council. **115**

13 July 1554 Assembly

fol. 17v.
116 Robert Myckelbarrowe finished his accounts and was allowed 20s 2d paid to Goodlake Chapman "for makyng of the pisse gote[6] on the west side of the water"; 13s 4d to Mr Hoode for Lady Suffolk's outrent; 4d to Wilkynson of Wiberton for outrent; 52s 3½d for twice riding to London for the town; and £4 for his fee. He now owes the town £42 9s 4d for last Michaelmas's rents.

117 Assessments set for payments for the repair of the parish church. John Fox, Robert Turpyn and John Harmon then Churchwardens.

118 If William Bogge agrees to become a freeman he is to be admitted to the Common Council.

119 Present: Lawrence Palmer, Mayor; Mr Tupholme, Mr Kyd, Mr Fox, Mr Parrowe, Mr Melsonbye, Mr Dobbes, Mr Johnson, Aldermen; William Smyth, John Goodale, Christopher Walker, Christopher Hix, Andrew Tompson, John Margery, Richard Draper, Bartholemew Grantham, Goodlake Chapman, Common Council.

9 October 1554 Memorandum

fol. 18r.
120 William Bogge took his oath as one of the Common Council before the Mayor, Mr Kyd, Mr Dobbes and Mr Melsonbye in the guildhall.

12 October 1554 Assembly

121 Agreed that Robert Myckelbarrowe should present his accounts on the 22 October in the guildhall before Mr Melsonbye and Mr Bryan.

122 Also Master Hoode should bring in his accounts on the same day or the day after before Mr Melsonbye and Mr Bryan, unless he has to go to London on the town's affairs, and then to account on his return.

123 All defaulters on the church assessment who continue to refuse to pay are to be called by a general citation. 13s 4d of this money is to be given to two persons to help ring the morning and evening bell, and he who "takyth the profit of the belles" also to ring.

124 Agreed that Mr Hood and Mr Forster shall ride to London on the town's business against John Browne, and for "the 50^{li} with the faculties, the revuyng of the councell letter for non pullyng downe of howses, and to speke with the lorde admirall for porters and measures".

[6] Sewer or drain.

Mr Meres to be consulted and retained as counsel for the town if available. 125

Present: Lawrence Palmer, Mayor; Mr Kyd, Mr Dobbes, Mr Parrowe, fol. 18v.
Mr Melsonbye, Mr Bryan, Aldermen; Stephen Clarke, John Goodale, 126
Christopher Hix, Andrew Tompson, William Smyth, John Eldrede, Christopher Walker, John Gawdrye, William Hawkrige, John Bell, Bartholemew Grantham, Common Council.

22 October 1554 Assembly
Agreed "that Mr Hoode and Mr Forster shall have a letter of Attornay 127
for and concernyng the Townes affayres at London before the Lorde Chauncellor and other the Kynges councell & ellswhere, and for John Brewers patent and other sutes, as for the councell letter agaynst pullyng Downe of howses, and for the reedyfying of howsen in Decay and ruyne and for the erection of the lands for l^{li} by the yere and other faculties with the forgyvenes or releasment of our Dett, and for certen sutes to the Lord admyrall concernyng the haven".

Agreed that Mr Forster and Mr Irby shall be the burgesses in the 128
Parliament for Boston, only Mr Bryan dissenting.

The consideration of Robert Myckelbarrowe's accounts deferred until 129
the Monday after All Saints Day.

Present: Lawrence Palmer, Mayor; Mr Kyd, Mr Fox, Mr Hoode, Mr 130
Dobbes, Mr Parrowe, Mr Sowthen, Mr Melsonbye, Mr Bryan, Mr Forster, Aldermen; Stephen Clarke, John Stevenson, John Goodale, Christopher Hix, Andrew Tompson, William Smyth, John Margery, Common Council.

23 January 1554/5 Assembly "by the aldermen"
"Old Kamock" of Lincoln to pay a fine of 2s for two cades of herrings fol. 19r.
which he bought before the price was set. 131

Agreed that "Nycholson the cost man and every other ship comyng a 132
lone, sholde lay uppe their heryng in a shoppe, and not sell the same to eny person, but to the fremen of the Towne, until more Stuffe come in, and a price thereof sett."

Present: Lawrence Palmer, Mayor; John Tupholme, William Kyd, 133
Robert Dobbes, Henry Fox, Simon Melsonbye, Thomas Sowthen, Robert Bryan, Aldermen.

31 January 1554/5 Assembly

134 William Bogge was admitted an Alderman and took his oath.

135 The house occupied by John Mason to be sold towards the payment of £100 to the Crown. John Mason promised to pay at 20 years purchase, plus an annual rent of 12d to the town.

136 The piece of ground called "the rose" also to be sold for the same purpose. Bartholemew Grantham agreed to pay £41 and an annual rent of 4d.

137 All freedom fines outstanding are to be paid immediately.

138 Agreed that Mr Hoode should be required to live in the town having been chosen a Justice of the Peace, and to bring in his accounts on Tuesday next.

139 Present: Lawrence Palmer, Mayor; John Tupholme, William Kyd, Henry Fox, Robert Dobbes, John Parrowe, Thomas Sowthen, William Bogge, Aldermen; Stephen Clarke, John Mason, John Goodale, Andrew Tompson, William Smyth, John Eldrede, Christopher Walker, John Gawdrye, Goodlake Chapman, William Hawkrige, John Bell, Bartholemew Grantham, Richard Draper, Common Council.

6 February 1554/5 Memorandum

140 After Mr Wendon's death Mr Hoode took his oath as Justice of the Peace 6 February before Lawrence Palmer, Mayor, and William Kyd.

9 February 1554/5 Assembly

fol. 19v. At this assembly a deed for John Mason's house was sealed and an
141 obligation for it delivered to Nicholas Harryman of Quadring, attorney, for Jenyt Webster of Deeping St. James.

142 Nicholas Harryman promised to bring a letter of attorney from Jenyt Webster for delivery of the deed.

143 Present: Lawrence Palmer, Mayor; John Tupholme, William Kyd, Harry Fox, Robert Dobbes, John Parrowe, Thomas Sowthen, William Bogge, Aldermen; Stephen Clarke, Andrew Tompson, John Goodale, William Smyth, John Mason, Christopher Walker, Goodlake Chapman, Bartholemew Grantham, John Gawdrye, John Bell, John Eldrede, William Hawkrige, Richard Draper, Common Council.

12 February 1554/5 Memorandum

Mr Hoode presented his accounts for his mayoralty which were held over until Christopher Hix's return from London. Present: Lawrence Palmer, Mayor; Mr Kyd, Mr Fox, Mr Dobbes, Mr Sowthen, Mr Parrowe, Mr Bogge, Aldermen. fol. 20r. **144**

22 February 1554/5 Assembly

The land called "the tile kylne grene" to be sold to John Browne for £15, plus an annual rent of 12d. **145**

Deed and obligation to Bartholemew Grantham sealed for the ground called "the Rose". **146**

Present: Lawrence Palmer, Mayor; Mr Kyd, Mr Fox, Mr Melsonbye, Mr Bryan, Mr Johnson, Mr Bogge, Aldermen; Stephen Clarke, John Mason, John Goodale, John Gawdrye, William Smyth, Christopher Hix, Bartholemew Grantham, John Margery, Goodlake Chapman, Common Council. **147**

25 March 1555 Assembly

At this Assembly Mr Kyd, Mr Sowthen and Mr Bogge were put in election for the mayoralty for the next year and by common consent Mr Bogge was chosen. **148**

William Wesname was chosen one of the Common Council. **149**

1 May 1554 [*sic*]

The names of the Aldermen and the Common Council and other officers when Lawrence Palmer entered the mayoralty: fol. 20v. **150**

Lawrence Palmer, Mayor.

Mr Tupholme, Mr Wendon, Mr Kyd, Mr Fox, Mr Hoode, Mr Dobbes, Mr Sowthen, Mr Parrowe, Mr Melsonbye, Mr Forster, Mr Bryan, Mr Johnson, Aldermen.

Stephen Clarke, John Stevenson, John Mason, John Goodale, Christopher Hix, Andrew Tompson, William Smyth, John Eldrede, Christopher Walker, John Gawdrye, Martin Bradley, Goodlake Chapman, William Hawkrige, John Bell, Bartholemew Grantham, John Margery, Richard Draper, William Bogge, Common Council.

Constables until Michaelmas next: William Tupholme, Bartholemew Grantham, for the west side; Francis Hartgrave, Richard Draper, Christopher Stamper, William Wadesworth for the east side.

Constables after Michaelmas: Roger Dowce, John Huntwike for the west side; William Crake, Christopher Lodge, Robert Symson, James Dowdike for the east side.

Dikegraves for the whole year: Thomas Deanes, Robert Worshoppe, John Gawdrye, William Wesname on the west side of the water; Christopher Walker, Robert Craythorne, Christopher Hix on the east side of the water.

15 March 1554/5 Assembly

151 Agreed that the Scottish ship riding "at the rodes" laden with Scottish herring shall be compelled to sell its cargo in the borough.

30 April 1555

fol. 21r. 152 Aldermen etc. when Lawrence Palmer, Mayor, left office: John Tupholme, William Kyd, Harry Fox, Robert Dobbes, Harry Goode, John Parrowe, Thomas Sowthen, Simon Melsonbye, Robert Bryan, William Johnson, George Forster, William Bogge, Aldermen; Stephen Clarke, Christopher Walker, John Stevenson, John Mason, John Goodale, John Gawdrye, William Smyth, Andrew Tompson, Christopher Hix, Bartholemew Grantham, John Eldrede, John Margery, Martin Bradley, William Wesname, Goodlake Chapman, William Hawkrige, John Bell, Richard Draper, Common Council. John Fox, John Harman, Robert Turpyn, Churchwardens.

marginal note "The pamplettes were myssyng when thes [following minutes] sholde have be wrytten"

27 February 1554/5 Assembly

153 Agreed that one barn and garth in the South End be sold to Alderman William Bogge for £13 19s 4d plus 4d a year outrent.

4 March 1554/5 Assembly

154 Deeds sealed: deed and obligation to William Bogge for his lathe and garth; the same to John Browne for "tyle kylne grene" in Skirbeck; grant to William Smyth of the purchase of his house and other properties for £43 plus an out rent of 12d a year; another deed for a tenement at "Skirbeck Gowt" worth 13s 4d per annum, sold to John Waddyngham.

fol. 21v. *blank*

11 October 1555 Assembly

fol. 22r. 155 Mr Leonard Irby and George Forster, gentlemen, are chosen burgesses in Parliament, offering to take no money for their service.

All the obligations due to the corporation by Master Paynell and Mr Lanttes shall be put in suit this Michaelmas term. 156

Sir Robert Richardson,[7] clerk, admitted to the vicarage of Boston. 157

Members of the corporation "shall come in a decent order in ther gownes like Townes men of such a corporacion at all tymes" at Assemblies at the guildhall, upon pain of 12d fine. 158

Ordered that "the weyght and mesures of the corporacion" shall not be borrowed without the license of the mayor and shall be kept in the Weigh-house; those borrowing them to pay the duty. 159

Leonard Bowshere, the mayor's clerk, to have, as clerk of the market, half of the perquisites of the office. fol. 22v. 160

21 October 1555 Assembly

"The same day it was agrede that the Charter of this Borrowgh whereby it is incorporatyde shalbe redd iiij tymes by the yere, that is to say on the Fryday in every imber weke in the guihalde at vij of the clocke in the mornyng in somer and viij of the clocke in the mornyng in wynter and then every of the xii & xviii to be ther presente uppon payne to forfete every of the xii that shall mysse xx^{d} and every of the xviii so making defawlte xii^{d}". 161

Further agreed "that all the company then beying in the hall, shall dyne together where the maior for the time beyng shall appoynte, and x^{s} of money to be allowed by the hall towards ther chargis and the remanent to be borne by the company". 162

26 October 1555 Assembly

A charter of incorporation for the cordwainers and curriers was sealed. 163

Leases granted to Annys Sympson, Simon Melsonbye, William Hawkrige, and William Crake. 164

13 December 1555 Assembly

William Spynk's former house "over agaynst the hall", previously sold to the corporation by his executors in settlement of a debt, to be sold to Thomas Sowthen for £40. fol. 23r. 165

[7] Robert Richardson, vicar, 1554–59.

166 Mr Palmer's account was approved and discharged.

7 January 1555/6 Assembly

167 Fine of 3s 4d to be laid on anyone allowing a "salte bytche" to go abroad. Lawful for anyone to kill such an animal and any owner attempting to prevent it is to be fined 20s or be imprisoned. This act to be proclaimed throughout the borough by the beadle once a year.

14 January 1555/6 Assembly

168 John Browne and Christopher Hix shall be attorneys at the next Term, answering for the town's affairs in London.

fol. 23v. John Dove shall be allowed to hold the parsonage of Boston, despite
169 the discharge of his lease for non-payment of rent, until Midsummer. If he then offers as much as any other for the lease he may have it; otherwise not.

170 Francis Hartgrave was discharged of the farm of the Grey Friars and the Bailiff sent to make a re-entry for the corporation.

25 March 1556 Assembly

171 "At this assemble communycacion was hadde for the office of the mayoraltie and at the last Mr Kyd were put in the election and so willed to go aparte which they dyd".

172 "And the same tyme by the hole comen assent Mr Kyd was chosen to be maior for the yere followyng, Who immediatly after ther callyng in and after the maior & the hole company had told hym ther goodwills towards hym praying hym to be contentid therwith dyd refuse to be the maior for the yere followyng and theruppon did tender his fyne for his refusall, which was xx^{li} yet by the intreatie of the hole company who dyd rather seke his goodwill in the service of the mairaltie for the yere folowyng, then the fyne of xx^{li}, he was at the lengyth well pleased to stand to the office of the mairaltie for the yere folowynge".

fol. 24r. Agreed by the whole company that the fine of £20 for refusing to serve
173 as mayor was too little, and the fine was increased hereafter to £40.

21 May 1556 Assembly

fol. 24v. Present: William Kyd, Mayor; Henry Fox, Robert Dobbes, Lawrence
174 Palmer, William Bogge, John Parrowe, Thomas Sowthen, Simon Melsonbye, Aldermen; Stephen Clarke, Andrew Tompson, William Smyth, John Gawdrye, John Bell, William Hawkrige, Christopher Hix, John Eldrede, John Mason, Bartholemew Grantham, Goodlake Chapman, Richard Kirkbye, Richard Draper, Common Council.

None of the Twelve or Eighteen to touch "the checke table"[8] upon pain of 12d fine. 175

The whole company to meet at the guildhall on Thursday in Whitsun week to view the accounts of Mr Dobbes, Mr Palmer, and Mr Sowthen. 176

Agreed that Mr Bogge, Mr Sowthen, Christopher Hix, Bartholemew Grantham and William Hawkrige should ride on Tuesday in Whitsun week to view the farm of Maltby alias Rayner. 177

The beam to be hung in the Weigh-house again and the weight and measures to be kept there. 178

Master Dobbes was elected one of the Justices and took his oath. fol. 25r. 179

28 May 1556 Assembly

Mr Sowthen allowed 21s towards his expenses for four journeys to London. 180

Mr Bogge, Mr Sowthen, Christopher Hix, William Hawkrige and Bartholemew Grantham reported on Rayner's farm at Donington. Mr Mayor is to deal with Rayner alias Maltby and let it to him by lease for as much money as he can get for the town's profit. 181

Agreed that John Margery have a lease of his dwelling house, stable and pasture for £3 3s 4d per annum. 182

11 January 1556/7

The bridge is to be repaired using the trees bought at Tattershall by Mr Fox. fol. 25v. 183

A patent is to be sealed for Mr Cecil[9] for 4 marks [? a year] and all arrears. Master Smyth is to be Recorder at a fee of 40s per annum. 184

Agreed that Mr Fox may purchase the pasture at the lower end of "Spayne Layne" for 40 marks. 185

Stevenson may have his pasture for £80, paying £20 down and the rest by annual instalments. 186

[8] ? the counting table.

[9] William Cecil (1520–98), 1st Lord Burghley, Secretary of State and later Lord Treasurer under Elizabeth.

20 January 1556/7 Assembly

187 John Browne is to obtain a citation to recover from the executors of William Brynklay the money "that by his will sholde remayne in the towne hall".

188 John Stevenson agreed to purchase his pasture for £80 paying the first £20 by Candlemas.

189 Deeds sealed for: Mr Fox's pasture; a lease for James Tomson; releases for Worshoppe and William Smyth; a letter of attorney for Christopher Hix and others; a patent for Mr Cecil.

March 1556/7 Memorandum

190 "The old bridge fell down this year the xxij day of Marche beyng Caryng Sonday or the Sonday before Palme Sonday between xi and xii of the clock of the same day".

25 March 1557 Assembly

fol. 26r. Thomas Sowthen, George Forster and John Parrowe were put in
191 election for the mayoralty and Sowthen was elected.

29 April 1557 Assembly

192 Francis Hartgrave is to be clearly discharged of the farm of the Grey Friars without further delay.

193 John Clarke, smith, was chosen as a bedeman.

30 April 1557 Assembly

194 Deeds sealed: for the pasture sold to John Stevenson; a lease to John Margery; a lease to Rayner alias Maltby; a lease to Christopher Lodge; a lease to Harry Felde; an obligation for Huntwike's children's parts.

10 May 1557 Assembly

fol. 26v. Agreed that for swearing "by the Masse or eny other othe, by eny
195 parte or membre of God in the hall or eny other place", an alderman is to be fined 2d and members of the Common Council 1d.

196 Discussion was held about making the new bridge and collectors appointed to gather money for it: William Wesname, Goodlake Chapman, John Stevenson, and Richard Kirkbye, for the west side of the water; John Mason, Christopher Hix, for "the myddell hollywater"; John Bell, William Hawkrige, William Smyth, for "the east hollywater".

Richard Dracott discharged as Serjeant and given 6s 8d as a reward. Richard Kelsay chosen in his place. 197

The Serjeants were discharged and readmitted to office and Kelsay took his oath. 198

1 June 1557 Assembly
John Bell and William Wesname were elected Aldermen and took their oaths. 199

28 June 1557 Assembly
John Parrowe, Simon Melsonbye, William Hawkrige, Robert Ditton, John Gawdrye and Richard Kirkbye were chosen sessors for raising money to set forth men to "the Lord Clinton, on the Kyng and Quens majesties affayres to Saynt Quyntyns".[10] The Constables ordered to collect the money. fol. 27r. 200

[*? June 1557*] *Memorandum*
"Abowte this present tyme the maior and Burgesses of this borrough dyde purchace to them and ther successors for ever, of the right honorable Lord Harry the Erle of Ructland all that his maner of Rossehall in Boston on the West side of the water with all the royalties perteyning to the same and certen pastures in Skerbecke quarter". 201

28 June 1557 Assembly [continued]
John Dove, being in arrears for a whole year's rent (£17) for the farm of the parsonage of Boston with the vicar unpaid, and owing other money to the town, is discharged of the farm. 202

3 July 1557 Assembly
John Dove is to bring in all the money and his acquittances due to the town for the parsonage and to have a decision on the matter at next Friday's assembly. fol. 27v. 203

9 July 1557 Assembly
John Dove is to pay to the town hall £26 13s 4d per annum for the parsonage for the remaining years of his lease, paying his rent from time to time, and also "dischargyng the vicker as before". He is to put in bond and take "no more customes or exactions of the parishioners then he hath done tofore tyme". The lease may be surrendered to the corporation on six months notice, Dove being compensated with 20 nobles a year for the remaining term of the lease. 204

[10] Troops sent to support the Spanish army attacking the French at St Quentin 1557.

15 September 1557 Assembly

205 Mr Nicholas Robartson was elected to the Common Council and took his oath.

21 September 1557 Assembly

fol. 28r. 206 Present: Thomas Sowthen, Mayor; William Kyd, Henry Hoode, Robert Dobbes, Lawrence Palmer, Simon Melsonbye, George Forster, John Bell, William Wesname, Aldermen; John Mason, William Smyth, Andrew Tompson, Christopher Hix, John Eldrede, John Stevenson, John Gawdrye, John Margery, Christopher Walker, Goodlake Chapman, William Hawkrige, Richard Draper, John Browne, William Crake, Richard Kirkbye, Robert Ditton, Common Council.

207 The corporation's part of a pair of indentures made 22 September 1557 with William Darby, John Browne, Richard Brigges and Thomas Johnson, executors of Thomas Browne of Fishtoft, deceased, is delivered to the executors on the receipt in the hall of the jewels, plate and ready money specified; these to be given up at such times as are specified in the indentures.

23 December 1557 Assembly

208 Christopher Hix, Bailiff, shall bring in his account next Thursday.

fol. 28v. 209 The collectors for the bridge money and the Constables collecting for the St Quentin expedition money are to bring in their accounts next Friday.

210 Robert Bryan discharged as an Alderman for his "none-habilytie"; John Gawdrye elected in his place and took his oath.

211 John Browne elected Alderman and took his oath in the place of Lawrence Palmer who died on St Andrew's eve.

24 December 1557 Assembly

212 Present: Thomas Sowthen, Mayor; William Kyd, Henry Hoode, Robert Dobbes, George Forster, Simon Melsonbye, John Bell, William Wesname, John Gawdrye, John Browne, Aldermen; John Mason, John Stevenson, John Eldrede, Andrew Tompson, Richard Kirkbye, Goodlake Chapman, Christopher Hix, William Crake, William Hawkrige, Robert Ditton, John Margery, Common Council.

fol. 29r. 213 Mr Leonard Irby and George Forster, gentleman, were chosen the burgesses at the next Parliament on 20 January 1557/8, taking no wages for their service.

4 March 1557/8 Assembly

Any of the Twelve or Eighteen absent from the Hall on any Friday in the Ember Week at 7 am in summer and 8 am in winter and for half an hour afterwards, though warned by the Serjeant, shall pay a fine of 3s 4d immediately into the box, unless he has the Mayor's permission to be absent. **214**

10 March 1557/8 Assembly

John Mason was elected Alderman and took the oath. **215**

John Fox, draper, William Dallands, mercer, Roger Bentley alias Dowce, shoemaker, and George Hallywell, draper, were elected to the Common Council. **216**

22 March 1557/8 Assembly

Robert Worshoppe was elected to the Common Council and took the oath, together with William Dallands and Roger Bentley. fol. 29v. **217**

The Bailiff and other collectors for the bridge money are to bring in their accounts next Monday afternoon. **218**

25 March 1558 Assembly

John Fox and George Hallywell took their oaths as members of the Common Council. **219**

George Forster, John Parrowe, and Simon Melsonbye were put in election for the mayoralty and George Forster was chosen by the whole assent of the house. **220**

28 March 1558 Assembly

Deeds sealed: a lease of a piece of waste ground in the manor of Hussey Hall to Goodlake Chapman for 12d a year; a lease of a piece of waste ground to Robert Worshoppe for 20d a year; a release to John Mason for two messuages in the market place; two patents to Sir John Mychell and William Neudyke, "for ther perpetual services duryng ther lyves", with fees out of the "erection landes". **221** fol. 30r.

14 April 1558 Assembly

Deeds sealed: a licence for Mr Hoode to dwell at Skirbeck until Michaelmas and keep his freedom; a licence to Richard Brigges to be a freeman of Boston and be discharged of all juries and petty offices; a letter of attorney to Leonard Bowshere to take possession of certain lands of Richard Brigges for the corporation. **222**

Mr Kyd's account for his mayoralty was approved and discharged.

Collectors of the bridge money made their accounts and were discharged.

fol. 30v. *blank*

6 May 1558 Assembly

fol. 31r. The seven Porters were sworn to the town's orders, which may be
225 amended by the Mayor and his brethren as thought fit.

226 "All the stuff" that passes from Mayor to Mayor is to be delivered by indented inventory, one part to be kept in the Hall.

227 "It is agrede that all the Aldermen of this Borrowe shall at all tymes in the Churche sitt in Our Ladys quere with the maior, or in the high quere on pryncipall feastes when the maior shall sett ther, uppon such paynes as in the howse shall be sett and taxed, And all the comen councell of this Towne to sit in the church in St Peters quere, on the north side thereof every hollyday from tyme to tyme on payne as aforesaide and so none of the howse to walke in the churche to the ill example of others".

228 William Odlyne, one of the Porters, took the freeman's oath.

2 September 1558 Assembly

229 George Hallywell may purchase his dwelling house for £35, discharging the town of the obit and paying 10s as an out rent.

23 September 1558 Assembly (Friday in Ember Week before Michaelmas)

fol. 31v. The outgoing Mayor henceforth is to make his accounts the Thursday
230 in Whitsun week after the feast of Philip and James, or be fined £10.

231 The Bailiff of the town's lands and rents is to make his account the Monday after the feast of [blank].

232 The Bailiff of the lands and tenements for the "new erection" is to make his account on [blank].

233 The Bailiff is to pay 20s to Mr Browne for setting out all the town's rents in a book.

Simon Melsonbye, John Browne, John Mason, Christopher Hix, William Hawkrige, William Smyth, and Richard Brigges, or any four of them, are to make an inventory of all the corporation's goods. **234**

17 October 1558 Assembly

Sessors for the latter payment of the subsidy[11] granted in Queen Mary's time were elected: Simon Melsonbye, John Parrowe, John Mason, Aldermen; Christopher Hix, Christopher Walker, William Hawkrige, Common Council; Robert Myckelbarrowe, George Erle, Robert Bonner, James Cherrye, Christopher Cooper, Edmund Toynton, Constables. fol. 32r. **235**

Mr Hoode's permission to dwell outside the town was extended until the feast of Saints Philip and James, he continuing a Justice and enjoying the liberties of the town. **236**

13 December 1558 Assembly

The will of Mr Nicholas Robartson the elder was brought into the hall from London; the copy cost 13s 4d. Mr Kyd brought in certain records of "the lord Roosse lordshippe", lately purchased, and the agreement for the vicarage. **237**

16 December 1558 Assembly

An ordinance made that "no person inhabityng within this borrowe, shall graunt or lett to eny forener, that is to say eny dwelling owte of this borrough that shall bryng wares (of what kynd so ever the same be) to the borrough ether bye lande or by water to be solde, any seller, shoppe howse or garth, within the same borrough, withowte the speciall lycence of the maior and the fowre justices of the said borrough, uppon payne to forfett for every such defawte done to the contrarye v^{li} (excepte the tymes of rakefayre, that is to say for the heryng men, and the towe fayres everye yere onlye)". fol. 32v. **238**

The warning of an Assembly left by the Serjeant at any man's house, he being in town, should be sufficient notice as if he spoke to him personally. **239**

12 January 1558/9 Assembly

Vicar Grene, lately chosen to be vicar of Boston, has renounced the presentation. **240**

[11] Probably the parliamentary subsidy or tax of one-fifteenth and one-tenth granted by Parliament in January 1558.

241 Deeds sealed: George Hallywell's assurance for his house, he sealing three obligations for £25; a patent to Thomas Merrycoke of £10 a year; a patent to Sir George Hankes of £6 13s 4d a year.

17 February 1558/9 Assembly (Friday in Ember Week)

242 Agreed that the common marsh at Wormgate End is to be let to the highest bidder and be enclosed from the highway. The money received is to be put in a common box with 3 keys, one held by the Mayor, another by one of the Common Council, and the third by the Dikegraves on the east side of the water. The money is always to be used about the common work of all the inhabitants on the east side of the water, "provided allway that theffecte of this acte shalbe unknytt uppe or fully agrede of to the maior come home".

19 February 1558/9 Assembly

243 Constables accounts presented: William Cartwright and Mathew Faceby owe 3s 3d; John Wilkynson and his fellows owe 13s 4d; William Dallands and Richard Robynson owe 9s 6d; Robert Worshoppe and Mr Sisterson owe 2s 4d. All these sums were paid to Christopher Hix and his fellow Dikegraves and the Constables were discharged.

fol. 33v. The Cordwainers brought in their accounts "for ther forfett money
244 among ther company" and paid the 3s 2d due to Mr Kyd.

6 March 1558/9 Assembly

245 Mr Kyd paid to Mr Mayor the 3s 2d for the Cordwainers.

246 Steven Mychell to be hired at £6 13s 4d per year and begin on Lady Day "so that he be here at the pryncipall feastes in the first Quarter".

247 The act concerning "the brode marshe" made on 17 February was read and approved.

248 Richard Foster is to have a lease of the little house and garth in the South end (formerly held by Harry Felde) for 8s a year.

20 March 1558/9 Assembly

249 All the beerbrewers are to sell double beer at 3s 4d the kilderkin and 20d the firkin, and single beer for 20d the kilderkin and 10d the firkin, and not above.

The porters are not to deliver coals (not belonging to freemen) out of any ship entering the port, either to freemen or foreigners without having the mayor's billet. Every foreigner is to pay 1d for a billet and the freeman nothing. 250

fol. 34r.[12]

John Jonson and John Dixon were elected to the Common Council and took their oaths. 251

No kidder is to buy fish in the market before 8 am in the summer and 9 am in winter, on pain of forfeiting the fish. 252

The "brode Marshe" shall be let at £4 per annum from Lady Day next. The town will fence it, the tenant paying 20s towards the cost. 253

25 March 1559 Assembly

Simon Melsonbye, John Parrowe and John Bell were put in election for the mayoralty and Simon Melsonbye was chosen. 254

1 May 1559 Assembly

fol. 34r.

John Browne, late alderman, "for that he by his owne tonge had Dyscharged hym selfe of his said Rowme", now discharged by the Mayor, Aldermen and Common Council and Nicholas Robartson, gentleman, elected Alderman in his place and took the oath. 255

19 May 1559 Assembly (Friday in Whitsun Week)

Mr Sowthen to have a lease for 21 years of all the lands in Wrangle that belong to the town. 256

Agreed that at Michaelmas next "ther shalbe towe chamberlaynes chosen owte of the comen councell, And they to gether all thet Townes rentes and to se that reparacions Done for one hole yere next, and then one of them to be put owte and an other of the same company to be chosen to serve in the same Rowme of a chamberlayne with the other that Remayneth still, so that every one after shall remayne in that office ij yeres shiftyng one every yere and they to have the Baylyffes fee, and by this maner every one (beyng chamberlayne before he be chosen to be an alderman) shall knowe all the lands that perteyne to this borrough". 257

At the same assembly Robert Wayde was chosen to be the town's Husband to see the labourers set on work and all things saved that belong to the borough. 258

[12] There are two folios numbered fol. 34.

59 A lease for 21 years granted to Mr Craycrofte of the void ground by the house he bought from Pynnell, and the adjoining tenement.

6 June 1559 Assembly

fol. 34v.

260 After discussion it was agreed to present "one Skarlyt otherwise callid Fiske"[13] to the vicarage of Boston, having £10 of the arrrears that will be due next Michaelmas.

29 December 1559 Assembly

261 Sessors for the tax payable to the Queen: Mr Bell, Mr Mason, Mr Parrowe, Aldermen; William Hawkrige, Christopher Hix, Richard Kirkbye, Roger Dowce, Common Council.

262 Constables chosen: John Dixon, William Lyname, Simon Turpyn, Harry Parker, John Gatlay, William Gayton.

22 February 1559/60 Assembly

fol. 35r.

263 John Stevenson agreed to purchase from the town one pasture for £80 and paid £20 down; his widow is unable to complete the purchase. Agreed that she have the pasture till next Candlemas which will be 4 years rent free, and be allowed the £4 10s owed by her to the Bailiff and also out rents due to the town (42s). But after Candlemas she is to quit the property.

264 Robert Myckelbarrowe is to be given £10 and 1000 bricks in return for his lease of the Austin Friars. And he may have the ground for one year from the feast of the Annunciation, paying the yearly rent. He is to bring in his lease when the £10 is paid.

8 March 1559/60 Assembly

265 Mr Leonard Irby was chosen a freeman, a member of the Common Council and an Alderman and took the oaths.

12 March 1559/60 Assembly

fol. 35v.

266 The Queen's Proclamation for abstinence from eating flesh in Lent and at other feast days was read and the following appointed as viewers: Mr Bell, Mr Mason, Mr Gawdrye, Mr Parrowe, Aldermen; William Hawkrige, Richard Brigges, Richard Kirkbye, William Smyth, Roger Dowce, George Hallywell, John Jacson, John Fox, Common Council.

[13] William Scarlet alias Fisk, vicar 1559–?71.

Agreed that unless Mr Hoode dwells in the town he should no longer be an Alderman. 267

Mr Carre is granted licence to take down the tan house. 268

Orkyng may have the lease of his farm but only according to the agreement made with him by Mr Kyd, Mr Sowthen and Christopher Hix. 269

Proposed that John Browne be the Town's Auditor at a yearly fee of £5 and to be bound in writing to the Mayor and Burgesses. 270

19 March 1559/60 Assembly
Francis Hartgrave is to go with certain members of the House to view what damage he has done at the Grey Friars. fol. 36r. 271

Deed sealed for John Wilkynson, mercer, for the purchase of his dwelling house at £40. This day he paid £13 6s 8d and made two obligations for the residue. 272

William Hawkrige was elected Alderman and took the oath. 273

William Tupholme and Thomas Thorye were elected to the Common Council. 274

25 March 1560 Assembly
Mr Bell, Mr Gawdrye and Mr Parrowe were put in election for the mayoralty and Mr Bell was chosen. 275

[*no date*] *1560 Assembly*
Agreed that Richard Brigges and John Dixon are to be Chamberlains of the town lands and have 40s each. To present their accounts the Monday after St Andrew's Day each year when one new Chamberlain shall be chosen. Thereafter each Chamberlain will serve for two years and be responsible for the town lands and the erection lands, paying the money yearly to the mayor. They are to instruct the town's Husband what reparations he should make. fol. 36v. 276

Christopher Hix and Richard Kelsay directed to make an entry into John Robynson's lands in the name of the Mayor and Burgesses. 277

17 April 1560 Assembly
Deeds sealed: for John Mason's purchase of a house in Bargate; for George Fayrefax's purchase of two pieces of void ground next to St George's Hall; a letter of attorney for entering John Robynson's lands. 278

fol. 37r. *blank*

fol. 37v. *1 May 1560 Assembly*

279 Mr Bell took the oath as Mayor.

280 The full company of Aldermen and Common Council is as follows: Master Bell, Mayor; Mr Leonard Irby, esquire, Mr Kyd, Mr Sowthen, Mr Nicholas Robartson, Mr Forster, Mr Melsonbye, Mr Wesname, Mr Parrowe, Mr Gawdrye, Mr Mason, Mr Hawkrige, Mr Johnson, Aldermen; William Smyth, Richard Kirkbye, John Margery, Richard Brigges, William Dallands, William Crake, Andrew Tompson, Christopher Hix, Roger Dowce, Robert Ditton, George Hallywell, Richard Draper, John Fox, John Jacson, John Dixon, William Tupholme, Thomas Thorye, Richard Robynson, Common Council.

27 May 1560 Assembly

fol. 38r. Charges for setting forth eight men for Berwick:[14] 2 pikes furnished

281 £3 4s; 3 harquebuses furnished 24s; 8 pair of hose £3 12s; 8 doublets 53s 4d; 8 jerkins 32s; 8 pairs of shoes 12s; 8 red caps 13s 4d; 8 sword girdles 8s; 8 "skerffs" 8s; 8 swords 26s 8d; 8 daggers 13s 4d; 8 "Rialls" for their conduct money £4; 2 Almayne Rivettes 30s; a bow, sheaf of arrows and stall 5s 6d; 2 bills 2s 8d; the Constables' charges 35s 2d. Total £24.

Sessors for levying the £24: Mr Parrowe, Mr Hawkrige, Aldermen; John Fox, John Margery, John Jacson, John Dixon, Common Council; William Gayton, William Lyname, Constables.

11 July 1560 Assembly

fol. 38v. Present: Mr Bell, Mayor, Mr Kyd, Mr Irby, Mr Dobbes, Mr

282 Sowthen, Mr Gawdrye, Mr Wesname, Mr Mason, Mr Hawkrige, Mr Brigges, Aldermen; William Tupholme, Richard Robynson, Thomas Thorye, John Fox, George Hallywell, John Jacson alias Wilkynson, William Smyth, Robert Ditton, Andrew Tompson, John Dixon, John Margery, Common Council.

283 Deeds sealed; a patent for John Browne's Auditorship of the borough and the £5 fee; an instrument for the non-residence of Mr Leonard Irby, Alderman, until next Candlemas.

284 The release and recovery from Mr Kyd and Master Forster of the lord Rutland's lands to Mr Melsonbye and Mr Mason for the town's use was brought into the hall.

[14] Part of an English expedition sent against the French in Scotland in 1560.

17 December 1560 Assembly
Agreed that the lease of a house formerly held by Mr Felde and now **285**
by William Hawkrige should be viewed to see who should bear the
charges [?of repairs]. It was thought to be in John Margery's hands.

[?] December 1560 Assembly (in Ember Week before Christmas)
Richard Brigges was elected an Alderman. **286**

John Wilkynson and John Stamper were elected to the Common **287**
Council.

The accounts of Mr Forster and Mr Sowthen are to be viewed the fol. 39r.
Friday after New Year's Day. **288**

Mr Gawdrye having made default forfeited 26s 8d for that he would **289**
not submit to the order of the House.

26 December 1560 Assembly
Sessors appointed for the tax: Mr Gawdrye, Mr Brigges, Aldermen; **290**
Thomas Thorye, John Jacson, John Fox, Christopher Hix, John
Dixon, William Smyth, Common Council; John Stamper, William
Rudder, Richard Jefferay, Robert Palmer, Thomas Willye, William
Halle, Constables.

13 January 1560/1
Christopher Hix's account for his bailiwick in 1558 was viewed and **291**
approved, the town owing him 12s 9d.

22 January 1560/1 Assembly ("Mr Maior and his brether")
The expenses of Mr Sowthen and Master Forster in London on the **292**
town's business shall be paid. They are to request Mr Leonard Irby
there to obtain counsel's opinion on John Robynson's lands and fol. 39v.
whether they may begin a suit against Mr Hunston over them.

28 February 1560/1
Persons appointed to make a new rate of tolls with "wharfage **293**
planeage and waying": Mr Bell, Mayor; Mr Sowthen, Mr Melsonbye,
Mr Johnson, Aldermen; Christopher Hix, John Wilkynson, William
Wesname, Common Council. They are to draw up the rate within six
days and present it in writing to the next Assembly for confirmation.

Mr Sowthen was fined 5s for "certen opprobryouse wordes" against ▽ **294**
Mr Bell, the Mayor.

7 March 1560/1 Assembly

fol. 40r. **295** William Tupholme is to be sold the piece of ground lately the lord Rutland's for 40s.

296 All unpaid bridge money to be levied and paid.

297 Agreed that Mr Wesname shall have a wall of bricks, certain foundations and tiles at the late White Friars for £5 and all reckonings owed him by the town to be discharged.

298 Agreed the new toll rates as follows:

"Imprimis for every pece of Rasons	1d.
Item for every pece of fygges	ob.
Item for every shippe or crayer ladyng or Dyscharging at eny of the Townes stathes beyng a foryner, to pay for Ryverage Kayge and plankage	2s
Item for every shippe being a freman	12d
Item lykewyse to pay for every kele	6d
Item for every pannyer of fresshe fysshe bowght in the markyt by any foryner or kydger	ob.
Item for every iij stone of chese bowght in the markyt by eny kyger	ob.
Item for every ij panyers of oysters	ob.
Item for every quarter of seame of mustylls	ob.
Item for every tonne of wares bowght owte of this lybertie, and passyng thorough the brydge and not Dyschargyng in the barrowe to pay	4d"

The new rates agreed by a majority of the House and to last until the feast of the Annunciation next. Those consenting: Mr Bell, Mayor;
fol. 40v. Mr Sowthen, Mr Melsonbye, Mr Wesname, Mr Mason, Mr Gawdrye, Mr Hawkrige, Mr Brigges, William Smyth, Richard Kirkbye, Richard Draper, John Dixon, John Fox, John Jacson, George Hallywell. Those not consenting: Mr Kyd, William Tupholme, Richard Robynson, Anthony Rawson, John Stamper, John Wilkynson, Thomas Thorye.

21 March 1560/1 Assembly

299 Agreed that Mr Bell or his assigns shall gather the tolls for one year from the feast of the Annunciation, paying rent of £20 for the year; and thereafter "to have the preferment before an other, and better chepe by xl^{s}".

The Austin Friars is to be closed in and let out at the best profit to the town. 300

Thomas Chapman being too sick to perform the office of Serjeant, he is to be granted a pension of 20s a year for the rest of his life. 301

13 April 1561 Assembly

John Dixon and his fellows, late Constables, presented their accounts for collecting the tax; they were in arrears by £3 6s 3½d which they paid and were discharged. 302

The Constables also accounted for the money collected for equipping the soldiers; they paid their arrears of 7s 11d and were discharged. fol. 41r. 303

Mr Bell the Mayor paid 31s 10d which he had received from Mr Derby for setting forth a soldier. 304

30 April 1561 Assembly

Letter of attorney to act for the town at London sealed for Mr Leonard Irby, Mr Sowthen, Mr Forster, and Christopher Hix. 305

Lease sealed to Robert Symson for his garthing. 306

The same day was delivered to Christopher Hix the charter confirmed by Queen Mary, the erection book also confirmed by her and the purchase book "that was purchased by Kyng Henry the viij". 307

Mr Kyd paid £3 18s 10d to the Mayor for his account of Lord Rutland's lands. 308

Mr Mayor also received: 14s 2½d out of the box for sealing money; £5 from Mr Melsonbye for his account for the late mayoralty; £11 from Mr Wesname for certain stones sold to him out of the White Friars; £12 from John Dixon and Richard Brigges, the Chamberlains, for their account ended at Michaelmas 1560; 18s 7½d out of the court box. 309

29 May 1561 Assembly

"At this assemble Christopher Hix brought in a letter from the councell for non pullyng Downe of the buyldyngs or eny howsyng in the borrowe which letter remayneth in Mr Maiors cubborde." fol. 41v. 310

Richard Draper brought in the charter for our commons in the "Erles Fenne". 311

312 The house where Richard Ditton dwelt is to be leased to one Lake, a wheelright, for 20s per annum.

313 The parsonage is to be leased to John Dove upon his giving sureties; and also the Austin Friars for £6 13s 4d per annum.

314 Richard Baxter of Wiberton is to be leased the farm where he is tenant for 20 years at a rent of 20s per annum and a fine for sealing the lease of 40s.

315 Four or five aldermen are to view the houses in St John's Row and make a book of their defects; to which John Dove should be bound.

30 September 1561 Assembly

316 Mr Melsonbye is to pay the Mayor the £10 that is due on his account and is then discharged.

317 Mr Bell shall present his accounts on a week's notice.

fol. 42r. "There was delivered to John Wilkynson nyne pownds in base money
318 as [—] slyppes by him agayne to be payde into the Hall at Christmas then next insuyng".

20 November 1561 Assembly

319 John Margery is to prove how he holds the lease that was Roger Wryghte's or be discharged.

320 Robert Myckelbarrowe is to show how he holds the lease of the house Gray lived in and also of the house that Wright lives in.

321 William Tupholme and Mr Sowthen are to bring in the leases of "Jerrarde Hall sellers".

322 Agreed that Mr Hawkrige, Mr Brigges, Mr Claymonde and William Smyth shall "viewe the castyng and fowyng of the Bardike, and sessyng the payment for the same, and Furthe to viewe howe it may be made to Rune, ebbe and Fludde".

323 Anthony Claymonde was sworn a freeman and after was chosen one of the Common Council and took the oath.

324 "No kydger nor carryer" is to buy any fish in the market before 7 o'clock in the summer or 8 o'clock in winter.

Every holy day the Aldermen are to attend church in Our Lady's Quire, and the Common Council are to sit in St Peter's Quire. Aldermen will be fined 12d and those of the Common Council 8d for non-attendance. 325

Agreed that when Mr Forster returns home the Hall or the Mayor shall request that he deliver up the town records. fol. 42v. 326

"The measures of the borrough both for lande and water shalbe viewed and maid accordyng to the statutes of this Realme". 327

Richard Robynson paid a fine of 20s for his bread being short weight. 328

Mr Sowthen agreed to pay £13 0s 2½d due on the account of his mayoralty. 329

Deeds sealed: bargain and sale to Anthony Claymonde of part of the manor of Hall Garth at a yearly rent of 11s 8d; deed by William Kyd, Simon Melsonbye and John Mason to Alexander Stoner for the purchase of a piece of land from the late possessions of Roos manor or Roos Hall, lying beside the Town House. 330

9 December 1561 Assembly

Mr Bell presented the account for his late mayoralty and was found to be £8 10s 11d in arrears which he promised to pay at the next Assembly. 331

Agreed that the "Holmes" shall at next Lady Day always be "the Rowght Pasture". 332

15 December 1561 Assembly

Agreed that the general Audit should be held on the Thursday in Whitsun week and that the Chamberlain or Bailiffs of the town lands and the late Mayor should then present their accounts. fol. 43r. 333

19 December 1561 Assembly

Mr Bell is fined 40s for his disobedience to the Mayor. 334

Thomas Thorye was chosen an Alderman and took the oath. 335

Richard Robynson, baker, one of the Common Council, was dismissed from the House for certain causes. 336

27 December 1561 Assembly

337 As regards Mr Hunston's demand for the Hall, its garthing, £10 a year of the erection lands and divers other things, for which he is going to law, he has now agreed to discuss the matter. Mr James Smyth, Mr Leonard Irby, Mr Melsonbye and Mr Browne are to have

fol. 43v. a letter of attorney under the common seal to treat with him.

338 Agreed that Mr Sowthen "for his unsemyng wordes gyven to Mr Maior, and for his disobedyence in certen thynges" shall pay as a fyne £3 6s 8d.

29 December 1561 Assembly

339 The letter of attorney for treating with Mr Hunston sealed and delivered to Mr Melsonbye.

340 Mr Bell paid his fine of 40s and had 18s returned to him.

341 William Gannocke and William Wadesworth were elected to the Common Council.

5 January 1561 Assembly

342 Agreed that John Jacson be Coroner.

343 Mr Claymonde was sworn chief Constable of this borough.

344 William Gannocke took the oath as one of the Common Council.

345 William Wadesworth paid the remainder of his freedom fine.

346 John Wilkynson paid the £9 he owed for the lease money "as slippes".

347 Scavengers chosen: George Erle for the east side of the water; and William Sisterson for the west side of the water.

fol. 44r. "This day were chosen to be Serchers for all handcraftes men within

348 this town to se them worke truly and to kepe at ther occupacion, Mr Mason, William Gannock and Richard Kerkbye"

9 March 1561/2 Assembly

349 Mr Forster brought in all the books concerning John Robynson's lands that Christopher Hix had taken up to London.

350 Searchers for those offending against the Queen's proclamation about the eating of flesh: Mr Hawkrige, Mr Brigges, Aldermen; John Jacson, John Wilkynson, Richard Kirkbye, George Hallywell, Common Council; Robert Covell, George Wilkynson, Leonard Smyth, John Lamand, Nicholas Fox, John Huntwike, Constables.

Mr Forster, giving up the office of Town Clerk to Thomas Doughtie or such other as the Mayor and burgesses shall appoint, is to have a yearly fee of 40s to be of counsel to the town. He is also elected Alderman in place of Mr Parrowe who is dismissed for non-residence. **351**

An alienation to be sued out at the next term for the lands that were once Lord Roos's in Boston. fol. 44v. **352**

Deeds sealed: to William Gannocke for two garthing places; to Christopher Mosse for a garthing "sted". **353**

16 March 1561/2 Assembly

Before this assembly Robert Bonner, Richard Jefferay and James Dandy, fishmongers, were committed by the Mayor and his brethren to the Hall or Counter "for that they wold not (on a wylfull mynd) scepe fysshe (as they before hadde) for servyng the markyt with such vittell as they occupied." This day the offenders referred their punishment to the order of the House. Bonner and Jefferay were fined 3s 4d each, which they then paid, and James Dandy 20d. **354**

Mr Mayor to propose the price of 20 marks and no less to Mr Craycrofte who wishes to buy his land and house that formerly belonged to Frieston Abbey. **355**

Mr Kyd and Mr Sowthen were both fined 40s "for takyng the fysshemongers partes agaynst the maior". Kyd's fine was remitted by the House; Sowthen paid his fine together with £3 6s 8d he had been fined on 27 December [1561], and this was then remitted by the fol. 45r. House except for 40s. **356**

John Stamper was fined 10s for "making Defawte in words agaynst Mr Sowthen" of which all but 2s was remitted. **357**

23 March 1561/2 Assembly

William Wadesworth took his oath as one of the Common Council. **358**

Mr Bell promised to bring in the chalice he has to the next Hall and the christmatories or the value of them. **359**

Robert Warde granted a lease for 60 years of the waste ground at the east end of the bridge towards the south end, leaving an adequate way for carriages and carts. He is to be given 20s for mending "the gollye mowth", is to remove the "gresynges next the side of the newe rentes" and is to pay 3s 4d per annum. **360**

361 William Tupholme paid 40s to purchase the garthing stede next to his house that was part of Lord Roos's lands.

362 Christopher Mosse paid 20s as part of the price for his garthing.

363 Mr Wesname is to buy the pasture under Stevenson's house, sometime part of Lord Hussey's lands, for 100 marks, paying 50 marks next Michaelmas and the rest the following Michaelmas. He paid 10s to Mr Mayor "for a godes pennye".

25 March 1562 Assembly

fol. 45v.
364 Mr Wesname, Mr Mason and Mr Hawkrige were put in election for the mayoralty and Mr Wesname was elected.

7 April 1562 Assembly

365 "Agreed that John Browne sholde conclude with George Allyne of London to be the Towne Clarke of Boston and so to take order with him that his lyving may be allway (one profyte with an other) the some of xx^{li} with the v markes that is his standyng fee, his howse rent the profittes comyng of his office and that which shall lacke to be made uppe with the perquisites of the courte of the clarke of the markyt".

366 Deeds sealed: the incorporation for the Company of Tailors; a lease to Robert Lake for the house he dwells in; to Mr Richard Craycrofte for his house and ground that was late Frieston abbey's; to Mr Wesname for the pasture behind Stevenson's house.

367 Received from Mr Bell the office found for Mr Fox's lands and the copy of his will.

fol. 46r.
368 Agreed that a letter should be sent to Mr Cecil asking his favour in securing from the Queen a licence in mortmain for lands worth £100 or 100 marks. He is to be given £20 and the charges of the licence are to be borne.

21 May 1562 Assembly

fol. 46v.
369 John Dixon presented his account as Town Bailiff for Michaelmas 1561 and was discharged.

370 Mr Sowthen is granted the farm of all the tolls within the borough by land and water, the profits of both the fairs and the market toll, "the damage phesant of the Brydge within this Borrough, the roughtes and the rought closse callid the Holmes" with all their profits, for one year at a charge of £30. A pair of gates is to be made for the bridge at the town's cost.

22 May 1562 Assembly

Deeds sealed: a letter of attorney to take possession of the erection lands; a deed for "Croston shoppe" at the old bridge end sold to Annys Fox, widow; a deed for John Wilkynson alias Jacson for Hussey Court house and another piece sold for 4 marks each. **371**

23 May 1562 Assembly

Agreed that all disputes touching the lands and tenements of John Robynson and other troubles between the borough and William Hunston, esquire, shall be settled according to such articles agreed and written in this book. fol. 47r. **372**

Those consenting to this agreement: Thomas Thorye, Mr Bell, Mr Brigges, Mr Hawkrige, Mr Forster, Mr Gawdrye, Mr Sowthen, Mr Dobbes, Mr Irby, Mr Kyd, Aldermen; Mr Mayor (two votes); William Wadesworth, William Gannocke, John Wesselhede, Anthony Claymonde, John Stamper, John Wilkynson, William Dallands, George Hallywell, Richard Kirkbye, John Jacson, Richard Draper, Robert Ditton, John Dixon, William Smyth, John Margery, Common Council. John Fox, Common Council, does not consent. Absent: Mr Melsonbye, Mr Mason, Aldermen; Christopher Hix, William Tupholme, Common Council.

The articles of the agreement follow on the other side [missing].

Gifts by certain persons towards the payment of £90 to Mr Hunston: Mr Anthony Claymonde £6 13s 4d (at next Christmas); Mr Kyd £10; Mr Bell 40s; John Stamper 10s. fol. 48r. **373**

28 July 1562 Assembly fol. 48v.

Mr Gawdrye's accounts for his mayoralty were approved. **374**

Mr Sowthen, Mr Melsonbye, Christopher Hix, John Wilkynson and John Browne are to examine and sort "all the bookes". **375**

3 August 1562 Assembly

The table for the toll and "damage phesant" was approved. **376**

13 August 1562 Assembly

John Dixon the Town Bailiff was instructed to distrain Alexander Skynner's ground for his out rent and the arrears of the same. **377**

John Margery brought in his lease of John Cooke's house in Conny Street to be viewed. **378**

14 August 1562 Assembly

379 Deeds sealed: to Mr William Hunston for a capital messuage, garthing and all the lands etc. in Walcot called "Stone thyng" or "toll

fol. 49r. thyng"; a letter of attorney to give possession of the lands; a bond of £300 by the Mayor and Burgesses to Mr Hunston to release to him all John Robynson's lands (except those in the town's possession); to Mr Hunston for a house and garthing lately held by Alexander Skynner and a letter of attorney for them; a patent to George Allyne and an indenture of his office as Town Clerk.

380 Thomas Wryght to be discharged of his house unless he can produce his lease.

381 William Wadesworth may purchase the house he dwells in and the "barbors howse" for £85, paying by instalments.

382 Richard Cocke may purchase the house he lives in for £40, paying by instalments.

383 Robert Palmer may purchase the house he dwells in with the house that Evers' wife occupies (excluding the kitchen next to John Mason's house) for £60, paying by instalments.

384 John Mason is to buy the above kitchen for £8.

fol. 49v. *17 August 1562 Assembly*

385 Richard Cocke paid £10 towards his purchase price of £40.

386 William Wadesworth paid £20 towards his purchase price of £85.

387 John Mason paid his whole purchase price of £8.

388 Robert Palmer paid £10 towards his purchase price of £40.

23 December 1562 Assembly

389 Agreed that the toll rate should stand and that a pair of gates should be made with speed.

390 Robert Ditton granted a lease of his garth in Fountain lane for 3s 4d a year, and a garth stede in Shodfriars Lane for 8d a year, and the cellar under the Hall for 40s per annum. Total 44s per year.

14 December 1562 [*sic*] *Assembly*

391 Elizabeth Farrar is to have her dwelling house and the kitchen and garthing lately in the tenure of Alyne Lodde for 21 years at 26s 8d per annum.

Andrew Leake is to have a 21 years lease of a house in the market place formerly held by Lownd and an orchard adjoining the Grey Friars for £3 a year. fol. 50r. 392

18 September 1562 [sic] Assembly
Thomas Scott granted a 21 year lease of a house with a garthing for 20s per year. 393

3 September 1562 [sic] Assembly
Anthony Claymonde elected Alderman and took the oath. 394

Richard Jefferay, William Stonehouse and Thomas Doughtie were elected to the Common Council. 395

The farm of the Tower and the pasture under it is let to Mr Sowthen for 21 years at £5 per annum, plus £5 for "an Income". He is to allow the Mayor and Burgesses to take down and carry away the gate house, they providing materials for the repair of the remaining building. 396

10 December 1562 [sic] Assembly
Deeds sealed: lease to Mr Sowthen for Hussey Tower and the pasture 397
for 21 years at £5 per year and a fine of £50; lease to John Clarke of a fol. 50v.
tenement with a garth stede near the Bar bridge for 21 years at 3s 4d per annum; lease to Robert Ditton of the cellar and two garth stedes for 21 years at 44s per annum; release to Anthony Claymonde of all the title in a house, buildings and 14 acres of pasture in Skirbeck in the tenure of Henry Hoode, and 5 acres of pasture near 'Kynges hyll' in his own tenure; deed to Thomas Thorye and his heirs for a piece of land with the appurtenances in Boston for 5 marks paid in advance; an indenture for Christopher Aresbye of his dwelling house for 20 years at 20s a year and a fine of 20s.

6 April 1563 Assembly
John Chester is to be sold a rood of pasture for £5. 398

Mr Mayor, Mr Sowthen, Mr Hawkrige, Mr Brigges, Mr Clement, Thomas Doughtie, Richard Kirkbye and William Smyth were appointed to survey all the town lands currently not leased. 399

Mr Browne, gentleman, is to pay a fine of 40s at the next assembly for "certen defawts and mysbehavors" towards Mr Mayor, Mr Sowthen, and Mr Dobbes. 400

15 April 1563 Assembly

fol. 51r. George Hallywell surrendered his lease of a house and 2 acres pasture

401 in the 'brode felde' and was granted a new lease for 10 years of 4 acres pasture called Mill Hill Green at 28s 8d.

402 The House bought an acre of land from Peter Margery for £6 to be paid at Michaelmas. This land is let to him together with 2 acres of pasture lately in the tenure of Edward Calverlay for 21 years at 30s per annum, plus a piece of ground before Peter's door for 2d a year.

403 Agreed that Mr Parrowe shall have 3 acres of pasture and 3 acres of arable land, as long as he continues in the town, for 30s per annum.

404 Thomas Gooddyng is to have his house and an acre of pasture for 24s rent.

20 April 1563 Assembly

405 Robert Wayde the gaoler is to be let the house he dwells in together with the long holmes "with all the rowghtes" for £7 a year.

fol. 51v. *blank*

4 June 1563 Assembly

fol. 52r. Any freeman acting against the liberties of the borough is to be fined

406 40s.

407 John Dixon is given an obligation of 40 marks of Mr Craycrofte and another of £5 of Robert Worshoppe.

7 August 1563 Assembly

408 Deeds sealed: lease to Andrew Leake; lease to Robert Warde for the ground at bridge foot; lease for George Hallywell; deed for John Chester of a rood of pasture.

409 Mr Wesname made his account for his mayoralty and was discharged.

410 John Dixon made his account for his bailiwick for 1562 and was discharged.

411 Mr Mayor acknowledged that he had received 40s from one Wilkynson of London "for goodes foren bowght and solde".

412 William Stonehouse was chosen as Coroner and took the oath.

The Constables are to present their accounts for "the last men that were sett forth" at the next assembly. **413**

Thomas Sowthen, Alderman, granted one little piece of ground at the north side of the west end of the bridge for 60 years at 4d per annum. fol. 52v. **414**

John Dixon to pay 20s to Master James Smyth due to him as his fee last Lady Day. **415**

blank fol. 53r.

blank fol. 53v.

25 May 1564 Assembly

John Dixon made his account as Town Bailiff and was found £25 8s 7½d in arrrears, which he paid into the treasury. fol. 54r. **416**

William Odlyne, porter, granted a lease of his dwelling house for 21 years. **417**

Mr Sowthen is to have £10 for his house in 'gawnt Layne' on condition he deliver up all the stuff belonging to it. **418**

John Dixon is to have a 21 year lease of his house, Stable Mill, and pasture at a rent of £4 per annum; the lease to be void if Dixon and his wife die before the end of the term and to revert to the Mayor and Burgesses. Dixon is to pay £10 for good will within 5 years. **419**

31 August 1564 Assembly

An order made forbidding the inhabitants to throw anything into the haven, above or below the bridge, on pain of 3s 4d fine on "the howse holde" for each offence and 3 days imprisonment for servants. Inhabitants are to keep their filth or dung until the Scavenger comes to their houses. fol. 54v. **420**

27 November 1564

Mr Wesname shall pay by instalments £8 13s 4d due to the town by his written obligation. **421**

22 December 1564 Assembly

John Dove is to leave the parsonage at Christmas without receiving any rents or tithes, but the town allows him all the money owed by him except for one quarter's wages which he must pay to the vicar at Christmas. **422**

9 January 1564/5 Assembly

fol. 55r. 423 John Dove is to be granted a 21 year lease of the ground called the Austin Friars at £6 13s 4d per annum. The Mayor and Burgesses are to build a house there for the tenant.

fol. 56–65r. *Summary of ordinances 1545–1593: omitted.*

fol. 65v–67v. *blank*

2 May 1567 Assembly

fol. 68r. 424 The collectors of the toll were summoned to pay their old rent and to put in sureties for next year's rent of £23 to be paid at Martinmas and Mayday.

425 John Clytherall and John Cossey, the Serjeants at the Mace, were discharged and then readmitted to office.

426 Mr Kyd, Mr Melsonbye, Mr Gawdrye, Mr Bell, Mr Brigges, Mr Wesname, Mr Claymonde and Mr Awdley were appointed to provide for the School house and to negotiate with Mr Townley for his lease.

427 Mr Awdley was appointed deputy to the Clerk of the Market.

428 "Also at the same assemblye it is agreid that all the shippes (beynge straungers or foryners) commyng to this Towne with eny kynd of vittelles, as coles salt fysshe corne fruttes or other lyke, shall bryng a
fol. 68v. say thereof to the maior of this Borrough, For the tyme beynge when they shall come for ther price, by such a measure as shalbe appoynted them by Mr Awdlay the clarke of the Markyttes debytie".

9 May 1567 Assembly

429 Everyone with a frontage on the Bardike is to scour and carry away the manure or filth before Trinity Sunday next. One side is to scour and the other to carry away, on pain of a fine of 12 pence per foot.

430 Mr Mayor is to appoint workmen to repair the bridge.

431 "Also yt is agreede that the viij^{s} payde to the Schole master towards the charges of his play shalbe allowed, and also the x^{s} that is gyven to the Wates of Cambridge".

432 Master Gannocke, Mayor, received 25s 4d out of the Court Box for the previous year during Mr Thorye's mayoralty.

No filth is to be thrown into the haven but placed where the following shall decree: Christopher Awdley, John Stamper, and Richard Draper for the east side; John Lanam and William Stonehouse for the west side. Defaulters to be set in the stocks or cage and their master to pay a fine of 3s 4d. **433** fol. 69r.

"None shall wasshe any clothes at the pumpes or within xxiiij foote of them, uppon payne to pay every defawte xij[d] by the view of John Fox and George Erle". **434**

19 May 1567 Assembly

Agreed "there shalbe a newe Scholehowse erected and buylded in the hall garth". **435**

21 May 1567 Assembly

Agreed that Thomas Thorye shall pay the £40 he owes on the account for his mayoralty in the following manner: £20 on St Botolph's day 1568 and £20 at Michaelmas 1568. **436**

John Wilkynson, Bailiff of the Erection Lands, presented his account for the past year, paid 13s 4½d that he owed to John Dixon the Town Bailiff, and gave up his office. **437** fol. 69v.

John Dixon, the Town Bailiff, presented his account for the town's revenues for the past year and was found to owe £23 13s 0d. **438**

William Hawkrige owes on an obligation to the Mayor and Burgesses £5 7s 3d. Money owed to him on a bill of charges is remitted and he is to pay £4 at Michaelmas 1568. **439**

23 May 1567 Assembly

According to ancient order the Charter of the corporation was read to the Mayor, Aldermen and Common Council. **440**

John Dixon presented his account of the rent received for the common marshes on the east side of the water ending at Michaelmas 1566 and owes 27s 2d. fol. 70r. **441**

6 June 1567 Assembly

William Wadesworth for his trespass was bound in £40 and his two sureties, Mr William Hawkrige and Mr Anthony Claymonde, in £20 each, for Wadesworth to appear when summoned before the Mayor and Justices. **442**

20 June 1567 Assembly

443 Bonds delivered "owt of the frame" to Mr Gannocke, Mayor: one of John Lanam for £10 due on St John the Baptist's day 1567; one of Christopher Cowper for £10 due the same day; one of William fol. 70v. Wadesworth for £10 due at Michaelmas 1567; and one of John Dixon for £3 6s 8d due the same Michaelmas.

21 July 1567 Assembly

444 A "clowe" is to be set at St John's bridge.

445 Mr Mayor, Mr Bell, Mr Gawdrye, Mr Melsonbye and Mr Claymonde shall view the ground that Robert Bryan wishes to sell to the town and decide whether to purchase it.

446 John Lanam paid £6 13s 4d due for William Lyname's house to John Dixon, the Town Bailiff.

447 William Wadesworth was dismissed from the Common Council "for certen causes movyng the hall".

448 Roger Cockes was chosen one of the Serjeants at the Mace.

449 The Churchwardens who are behind with their accounts must present them on 15 August or be fined 6s 8d each.

450 John Lanam's bond of £10 was delivered to John Dixon.

fol. 71r. Memorandum: Mr Mayor retains Richard Draper's bond made for
451 the performance of the covenant of his indenture.

452 Agreed that Mr Mere's patent should be sealed.

7 August 1567 Assembly

453 Agreed "that every Alderman and al they that be of the comen councell shall attende uppon the maior for the tyme beyng on sanct george Day and on sanct James Day, accompanying hym first to the Crosse and so into the beast markyt untill the proclamacion be maid and done, and from thence to the guyhalde, and ther to remayne untill the court be endyd and Dissolved" on pain of a fine of 3s 4d for an Alderman and 20d for one of the Common Council.

454 Mr Claymonde fined 20s "for undecent workds [sic] contrary to the ordynaunces of the howse".

John Lanam committed to prison "for the undecent orderyng of hym selfe"; released on payment of a fine. 455 fol. 71v.

Denis Robynson sent to prison for drawing his sword against the law, being a Constable; later released pending a further trial. 456

19 September 1567 Assembly

George Forster is to be the Town Clerk and have the customary fee. 457

Sessors for the tax appointed: the Constables, and John Fox, John Wilkynson, William Dallands, Richard Felde, and William Stonehouse. 458

19 December 1567 Assembly

Agreed that John Dixon, Bailiff, is to pay to Robert Dobbes 20s owed to his late father Robert Dobbes, Alderman. 459

12 January 1567/8 Assembly

Agreed that the property given to the corporation by Richard Brigges (after the death of him and his wife Audrey) shall be used to support an usher in the grammar school at Boston for ever. fol. 72r. 460

Deeds sealed: lease for 10 years to William Gannocke of 16 acres of pasture at Wiberton at £5 per annum; lease for 21 years to Richard Brigges for two pastures in the holmes in Boston at £3 13s 4d; a feoffment by Richard Brigges to William Derby, Robert Townley and Christopher Brande of a messuage and lands in Toft, Boston and Skirbeck; a deed to John Lanam of a messuage called "the grete head" in Boston for £26 13s 4d. 461

Agreed that Dorothy Mason, widow, shall be let 12 acres of pasture that she had of Mr Fox deceased, for £5 per annum "and she to bear all charges and not to be put away, Withowt a reasonable cawse or marrye". 462

John Lanam stands surety for William Smyth to pay his half year's rent of £5 15s 0d on Mayday. fol. 72v. 463

John Lanam is to pay 6d a year for a piece of ground that he has enclosed with his wall on the south side of St George's hall. 464

Christopher Awdley ordered to pay 12d at the next assembly for leaving without permission before the end of the meeting. 465

466 Mr Sowthen having agreed to give up his lease of the marshes to the corporation on Lady Day, he shall be granted a new lease of 21 years at £7 per annum "towardes the fyndyng of an ussher in a grammar Schole in Boston", provided that he allow the inhabitants to drive their cattle through there in winter.

467 Mr Hawkrige has agreed likewise and to pay 40s a year.

468 "Item it is agreed at this assembly that all the xij aldermen of this Borrough that have bene Maiors, shall were there Tippettes of velvet and ther Liveray gownes of these Days folowing, as well in the church
fol. 73r. as in the stretes, that is to say of thannunciacion of our ladye, Ester Day, Maidaye Sanct george day sanct James Day, Whitsonday, allhallowe Day, christmas Day and xii^{t} Day uppon payne of every man makyng Defawt ij^{s}".

469 "Item it is agrede that for the settyng of the pore people of this Borrough in labore & worke that every one of the xii^{t} aldermen shall delyver xx^{s} a pece, and every one of the comen councell shall delyver x^{s} a pece to suche person or persons as shalbe therunto appoyntyd to have the settyng of the pore on worke, And at the yeres end every man to be answeryd his money agayn by the said overseers, And it is agreid that Mr Claymond, Mr Awdlay and John Stamper shall gyve thaccompt for the same, and to be the overseers."

12 March 1567/8 Assembly

470 George Forster of Boston appointed Town Clerk for life and took the oath.

471 William Stonehouse was dismissed from the Common Council and from his freedom, because he dwells out of the liberty.

fol. 73v. William Derby, esquire, was admitted a freeman and took the oath
472 and was then elected to the Common Council and took the oath.

473 Andrew Leake was elected to the Common Council.

474 "James Kay clarke[15] was appoyntid to serve the Maior & burgesses in preaching and otherwise according to the last will of Henry Fox Dysceassed, and that he shall have x^{li} a yere and meate and drynke."

[15] James Kay, mayor's chaplain 1568–72.

John Dixon and George Erle were appointed Bailiffs and collectors of the town rents for the next year and allowed £4 for their pains between them. **475**

15 March 1567/8 Assembly

Andrew Leake took his oath as a member of the Common Council **476**

William Derby, esquire, was elected an Alderman and took the oath. **477**

fol. 74r.

Richard Brigges, Anthony Claymonde, William Hawkrige, John Stamper, John Wilkynson and Christopher Awdley, or any four of them, are appointtted for a year to sell such of the town's houses as they see fit. **478**

George Claymonde, gent., may buy back all the land at Wiberton that he sold to the town, paying £40 on 14 September and £18 at Mayday 1569. The town to receive the rents due at Mayday next or 30s in lieu. **479**

Maud Foster to have two cellars, one cottage and three acres of pasture for her life for 49s 8d per annum. Christopher Awdley stands surety for her bound in the sum of 20 marks to pay the town £10 within one month of her death. **480**

23 March 1567/8 Assembly

Mr Lawrence Meres, esquire, was admitted a freeman and took his oath and his fine was remitted. **481**

fol. 74v.

Mr Meres was admitted to the Common Council and took the oath; he was then elected an Alderman and took the oath. **482**

Robert Bonner was elected to the Common Council and took the oath. **483**

Agreed that the executors of William Kyd, late Alderman, may have liberty for them and their workmen to build a cross on the common cornhill on the east side of the water, according to Kyd's direction. The cross once built is to be repaired by the town. **484**

25 March 1568 Assembly

John Bell, Alderman, was nominated and elected Mayor. **485**

17 April 1568 Assembly

fol. 75r.

George Allington, gent., was appointed the town's deputy to present their accounts to the Exchequer. **486**

487 The same George Allington was granted an annuity of 20s to be paid at Michaelmas and Lady Day.

488 Thomas Sowthen, William Derby and Anthony Claymonde, Aldermen, Christopher Awdley, John Lanam, Andrew Leake, William Dallands, and Richard Jefferay were appointed to examine the accounts for the building of the new school house and found the charge came to £195 0s 11d.

fol. 75v. Thomas Sowthen, Alderman, was granted a little piece of ground at
489 the north side of the west end of the bridge for 60 years at 4d per annum.

490 John Dixon is to pay Master James Smyth 20s which was due to him as his fee last Lady Day.

fol. 76r. *blank*

3 May 1568 Assembly

fol. 76v. Agreed that the corporation "shall deliver into the lottery[16] the some
491 of xv^{li} to be put in the name of the maior to thuse of the borough".

492 Several inhabitants agreed to put certain sums into the lottery: Robert Bonner "shall bere the name for all their parts & to be equally Devided emongest theym if any guid fortune channce".

493 At this Assembly William Gannocke, late Mayor, delivered to John Bell, now Mayor: the account of John Browne; one bill of debt of £17 owed by William Wesname, late Alderman; an acquittance for the payment of the last tax; a bill of debt of 26s 8d due by Melchior Smyth of Hull; the Queen's writ of *diem clausit extremum post mortem* concerning William Tupholme; a letter from Lord Willoughby to the Mayor and Burgesses concerning David Ward, clerk; the Queen's writ of *capias ad satisfaciendum* against William Wadesworth at the suit of Richard May of London for a debt of £33 6s 8d.

8 May 1568 Assembly

494 Mr Fisk, vicar of Boston, owes £7 of "old dett", in addition to £9 due to the Queen according to the accounts in the Exchequer, which the town is charged with levying. Agreed to deduct 60s from his wages each quarter until the debt is paid.

[16] An early state lottery with the proceeds being used to repair havens.

10 May 1568 Assembly

William Smyth is to have 20s per annum by patent for life, to be paid by the collectors of the town's revenues. fol. 77r. **495**

William Smyth and Thomas Chapman surrendered their office of toll gatherers. **496**

17 May 1568 Assembly

The executors and supervisor of the will of Agnes Fox deceased who bequeathed goods and chattels to the poor people of Boston are to make a full account of the goods deducting all necessary expenses. The residue owing to the poor shall be delivered to the Mayor and four J.P.s when the account is presented next Thursday. The Mayor and J.P.s are to put in a bond to the executors discharging them of all demands arising out of the will of Henry Fox or Agnes Fox. **497**

Ordered that "towchyng the conveying and bringyng of Freshwater from Kele hill to this Borough of Boston that there shalbe foure of the Aldermen viz Mr William Derby Mr John Gawdre Richard Brigges and Antony Cleymond And foure of the common councell viz Jeffrey Woyze John lanam Richard Draper & Andrewe leeke that they viij shall consider howe & by what meanes the same Water may be brought to this Borough And what everymans benyvolence wilbe graunted to the same And thereupon to certifie this howse of theire Doyinges and procedinges therein With asmoche spede as they may reasonably Doo". **498**

Alderman Richard Brigges was sworn in as a Justice of the Peace. **499**

21 May 1568 Assembly

The following persons were absent, having been warned: John Gawdrye, William Hawkrige, Aldermen; John Lanam, William Dallands, Andrew Leake, Common Council. fol. 77v. **500**

10 June 1568 Assembly

The account of John Dixon, Bailiff, was taken before the Mayor and his brethren, and he owes £11 14s 8d, as well as one bond for £10 owed by John Lanam and now in dispute. **501**

Mr Mayor delivered a general acquittance for Mr James Smyth's fee, due last Lady Day. **502**

11 June 1568 Assembly

503 The following bills and bonds were delivered to Mr Bell, Mayor: a bill of debt of William Wesname for £17; a bond of Thomas Doughtie and others to pay £4 at the Purification of Our Lady 1567; a bond of Anthony Claymonde for £30 payable at Michaelmas 1567; a bond of [—] Smyth of Hull, clerk, and vicar of [—] for 26s 8d; and a bond of John Lanam and others for the payment of £10 at Christmas 1567.

504 Ordered that the matter of the bond of £10 due by John Lanam and now in dispute between William Gannocke and John Dixon be
fol. 78r. referred for trial and decision to the next Assembly.

505 Licence sealed for Robert Townley, Robert Bonner and Richard Jefferay to erect a wooden frame in the market according to the will of Alderman William Kyd deceased.

506 The accounts of John Dixon and William Gannocke, late Mayor, were taken and the sums they owe appointed.

507 John Browne owes about 40s on the suits of the town; it is to be allowed to the town out of his fee next Michaelmas.

508 John Wilkynson is owed 65s 9½d on the Church account; he has received 100s of the debt of Mr Woodruff, schoolmaster, and has paid 33s 2½d to Mr Mayor and so is charged.

509 Richard Mykelbarrowe shall have the collection of the tolls in Boston on May Day next for a yearly rent of £23, subject to the order of the House whether he is to continue next year. He is to put in sufficient sureties at the next Assembly.

510 John Bell, Mayor, delivered to Thomas Doughtie a bond of £4 due at Candlemas next.

511 Richard Draper, farmer of the parsonage of Boston, is to "trye" with the parson of Coningsby at his own charge whether Armtree fen is part of Coningsby parish.

17 September 1568 Assembly

fol. 78v. Alderman William Derby, esquire, delivered to John Bell, Mayor,
512 four bills for the lottery containing 63 lots at 10s each. 30 lots were for the corporation and 33 for the following inhabitants: Alderman Leonard Irby, esquire, 2 lots; Alderman John Gawdrye 1 lot; Alderman Simon Melsonbye 1 lot; Alderman Richard Brigges 1 lot; Alderman Thomas Doughtie 1 lot; George Forster, Town-clerk, 1 lot;

Alderman Thomas Thorye 1 lot; Alderman William Gannocke 3 lots; Alderman William Derby, esquire, 1 lot; Alderman John Bell 1 lot; Anthony Kyme, gent., 2 lots; Alderman Thomas Sowthen 2 lots; Christopher Awdley, gent., 2 lots; Robert Bonner 1 lot; John Wilkynson 1 lot; George Erle 1 lot; William Dallands 1 lot; Richard Jefferay 1 lot; Richard Draper 1 lot; John Dixon 1 lot; John Fox 1 lot; Philip Curtes 1 lot; Jeffrey Ware 1 lot; Andrew Leake 1 lot; John Lanam 1 lot; Richard Felde 1 lot; Alderman Anthony Claymonde 1 lot. Total of all the 33 lots is £16 10s. Received by the hands of Thomas Seynt Poll, esquire, 10 September 1570, £4 18s 6d.

4 October 1568 Assembly

Robert Bonner, executor of William Kyd, delivered and sealed a deed of gift to the Mayor and Burgesses of a messuage commonly called "Goche Houwse or Merycockes Howse" where William Pylowe now lives which William Kydd gave to them 18 May 10 Eliz. fol. 79r. **513**

By deed dated 12 April 1568 the corporation granted to William Bond two cottages and two tenements being built on the south side of the haven now in the occupation of John Rynger and [?An] Lee. **514**

9 October 1568 Assembly

Anthony Claymonde, gent., is to have assurance of a messuage in Boston where Roland Bell lives on payment of £10 by instalments. **515**

George Erle received £31 from Anthony Claymonde, gent.; £26 for his arrears and £5 towards the purchase of Bell's house. **516**

Agreed that Mr Mayor and Mr William Derby shall negotiate on behalf of the corporation with the Sewer Commissioners for an agreement that fresh water may be conveyed out of Hildyke to the borough. fol. 79v. **517**

15 October 1568 Assembly

William Hawkrige paid £4 due on the account of his mayoralty and received his bond for the debt. **518**

William Gannocke paid £32 10s due on the account for his mayoralty and received his bond for the debt. **519**

George Erle paid £26 on behalf of Anthony Claymonde, gent., which was due for his mayoralty and for the purchase of Bell's house in Southend and received the bond for the same. Memorandum that Anthony Claymonde had owed £30 on his mayoralty account but was allowed £4 for 2,000 "thack tile" delivered to John Dixon for the school-house. **520**

521 John Bell, Mayor, paid £10 on behalf of Christopher Cowper and received the bond for the debt.

fol. 80r.
522 John Bell, Mayor, paid £20 on behalf of Thomas Thorye, late Mayor, due for his mayoralty and received the bond for the same.

523 John Bell, Mayor, paid £15 on behalf of Thomas Wright for the purchase of his house.

524 John Browne received a bond in which he and James Smyth, esquire, were bound to the corporation for £40 which was paid long ago.

525 William Gannocke received acquittance for his mayoralty in 1567 from John Browne the auditor of his account.

5 November 1568 Assembly

526 Agreed that the diking of the new drain to Cow Bridge shall be done with all speed. John Bell, Mayor, is authorised to spend 20 marks on it.

9 November 1568 Assembly

527 Richard Draper, lessee and farmer of the rectory of Boston, is allowed £7 from his year's rent for repairs he has made to the "high Quere"; he paid the remaining £8 to the corporation.

fol. 80v.
528 John Bell, Mayor, Simon Melsonbye, Richard Brigges, Anthony Claymonde, John Lanam, Jefferey Wouze and Andrew Leake or any five including the Mayor, are authorised to sell all such messuages, cottages, cellars and stables under a commission subscribed by Mr Lawrence Meres, John Gawdrye, Thomas Thorye, William Gannocke, William Dallands, Christopher Awdley and Richard Felde.

18 November 1568 Assembly

529 Mr Bell, Mayor, Thomas Sowthen, Simon Melsonbye, William Hawkrige, and Anthony Claymonde with the assistance of the dikegraves are before St Andrew's day next to make a "trewe perficht and certen acre boke of all the landes off the Est side of the water" listing each charge for all those chargeable for making and repairing the sea banks there. They are to certify this to the corporation in writing which shall remain in the Guildhall for perpetuity.

17 December 1568 Assembly

530 The following defaulted contrary to the ordinances: William Gannocke, Alderman; John Margery, Philip Curtes, Thomas Owresby, George Erle, Common Council.

31 December 1568 Assembly

In Michaelmas term the late sheriff of the county of Lincoln John Copledike, esquire, directed his precept to the Mayor and Burgesses of Boston according to the Queen's writ for the arrest of Thomas Sowthen, Alderman, to answer an action of trespass brought by William Candisshe, esquire, in the Queen's court. The said Thomas promised the Mayor and Burgesses to discharge them for the said return. fol. 81r. **531**

One obligation in which William Wadesworth and William Dallands stood bound to the Mayor and Burgesses in £20 dated 7 March 1565/6 . . . [incomplete] **532**

Agreed that Walter Woodruff, clerk, schoolmaster of the borough, may pay the 100s he owed to the Mayor and Burgesses at Christmas last on Lady Day. **533**

Agreed that Richard Draper, farmer of the parsonage, shall be allowed all the sums of money he can prove he has paid to William Fisk, clerk, vicar of Boston, for his wages now and in the future. **534**

Christopher Awdley, gent., one of the Eighteen, is to be the Mayor's deputy as Clerk of the Market. fol. 81v. **535**

11 January 1568/9 Assembly

"First it is agreed that no maner of person beyng appoynted as a Tipler within this Borough shall sell aither in his howse or out of his howse any countre ale other then suche as it at this assemble are appointed and assigned. viz **536**

William Lynn	William Pilowe
Thomas Godding	Richard Child
John Cartwright	Robert Barnes

upon payne of anyone makyng defalt iii^{s} iiij^{d} for every tyme offendyng".

"Also it is agreed that no maner of person shall sell aither in his howse or out of his howse any bere brued out of this Borough upon payne of every person making default iii^{s} iiij^{d} but suche as is hereafter named and appoynted. Viz Peter payntre Thomas Browne". **537**

"And for the good order therein to be hadd and performed it is agreed that John Gateley Charles Brandon and William Whitwong to present theym that do use themselfs to the contrary". **538**

27 January 1568/9 Assembly

539 All articles, sentences and clauses in the indentured writing made between the Mayor and Burgesses and the Warden and Fellowship of the mystery and occupation of glovers and white leather tawers dated 23 December 1568 shall stand in full force during the pleasure of the corporation.

fol. 82r. Whereas William Fisk, vicar of this borough, is indebted to the Queen
540 and the corporation in the sum of about £20, the corporation will pay the Queen's duty on the vicar's behalf, deducting from his wages 30s a quarter until all the money owed to the corporation is paid.

21 February 1568/9

541 Richard Feilde was chosen Coroner and took the oath.

4 March 1568/9 Assembly

542 At this Assembly William Dallands purchased his dwelling house in the market stede and the adjoining shop in the tenure of William Sisterson, one shop in the tenure of William Dixon, and one shop or backhouse in his own tenure with all the shops and casements, for £100 to be paid in instalments and an outrent of 4d yearly due on Lady Day.

543 Richard Draper is to be given until Michaelmas to pay the £8 due upon his bond for his rent payable at Lady Day.

fol. 82v. Peter Fry has purchased one stable and one yard abutting upon the
544 haven late in the tenure of John Margery for £7 to be paid at Michaelmas next and a yearly outrent of 1d due at Lady Day.

9 March 1568/9 Assembly

545 "Att this Assemble it is agreed that Cristofer Awdeley and Dyonise Robinson shall ride to Norwiche And there to view and peruse howe and aftur what maner certen Fleminges and other straungers be used and occupied there in theire faculties and occupacons to thentente that certen Fleminges and Straungers lately commen into Boston may be sett on worke by means of suche straungers as the said Cristofer and Dyonise shall move to come to Boston And to have toward theire charges xl^{s}".

546 Confirmation of the order that anyone refusing office of mayor be fined £40.

22 March 1568/9 Assembly

547 The charter and purchase book from King Henry VIII was brought from London and put in the "Frame".

William Colman, tailor, and William Peycock, tailor, were admitted freemen. They are to pay 20s each by instalments. **548**

George Claymonde, gent., shall be bound with sureties to pay to the Mayor or Bailiff £21 10s at Michaelmas, £20 the next Michaelmas, and £20 at Michaelmas 1571. The town is to receive the rent due at Lady Day and assure Claymonde all the lands in Wiberton previously bought of him. **549**

25 March 1569 Assembly

Thomas Doughtie, Lawrence Meres and William Derby were nominated for the mayoralty and Thomas Doughtie was elected. fol. 83r. **550**

31 March 1569 Assembly

Thomas Sowthen, Alderman, acknowledged a recognisance of £40 to appear at the Guildhall in Boston before the Mayor, Aldermen and Common Council on Friday after Low Sunday. **551**

4 April 1569 Assembly

Andrew Leake is elected Bailiff for two years in the place of John Dixon. **552**

Agreed to discharge Robert Wayde of his office as Gaoler and of the house where he lives. **553**

Richard Feilde, John Margery, Richard Draper, Thomas Owresby, and Robert Bonner, Common Council, defaulted at the Asssembly. **554**

14 April 1569 Assembly

Agreed that the obligation of Mr John Browne should be left until further order is made concerning the goods of Agnes Fox, widow. fol. 83v. **555**

The following were absent from this Assembly: John Gawdrye, William Hawkrige, Aldermen; John Margery, William Dallands, Common Council. **556**

Anthony Claymonde and Richard Draper, Surveyors of the High Ways,[17] are to employ during the next year "all the men worke dayes of the Inhabitauntes" to make the new drain and repair the adjoining highway. **557**

[17] Surveyors of the Highways responsible for road repair were authorised by statute in 1555.

22 April 1569 Assembly

558 "First Whereas Thomas Sowthen one of the Aldermen and Justice of this Borough before this tyme did departe out of this Borough with his wiff servauntes and famylie and with his howse hold stuff then myndynge and intendyng to inhabit and dwell at Peterborough without licence of the Maior and Burgesses of Boston contrarie the Kings charter And contrarie to the orders and lawes heretofore made Never the lesse the same Thomas Sowthen beyng called in this assemble before the Maior and Burgesses hath submytted hym self to the said Maior and Burgesses to stand to theire order where upon the same Maior and company are content to remyt that his offence of departure upon condition that he shall make his abode within this said Borough and execute his office of Aldermanship and Justice of Peace accordynge to the Kings charter graunted to this Borough by the Kyng of England, King Henry the viij and the ordenaunces constitutions and laws of this Borough."

fol. 84r.
559 "Also it is agreed at this assemble that William Derby squier, one of the Aldermen of this Borough shall move master Secretary Cicill and knowe his pleasure whether the Maior and Burgesses may lawfully suffre certen straungers to Inhabit and dwell within this Borough with out daunger of the Quenes lawes".

29 April 1569 Assembly

560 "First it is agreed that the Bakers and Brewers of this Borough shall have licence in writyng under the Comon Seale of this Borough to be a comonaltie of theym selfs for the mayntenaunace and good order to be observed and kept by the same Bakers and bruers for the Common Welth of theym selfs and the Inhabitants of the same Borough accordyng to certen articles mencioned in the same writyng . . ."

561 By deed of 9 October 1568 the Mayor and Burgesses grant to Robert Bonner of Boston, fishmonger, one piece of land in Boston "lying as well upon the Est part as of the west part", abutting upon the common way to the north and upon Robert's land to the south, as part of the town's Manor of Halgarth in free socage or burgage with suit of court to the borough twice yearly, together with a letter of attorney to Leonard Bowshere, clerk, and Richard Jefferay.

fol. 84v.
562 Deed of bargain and sale to William Dallands of his present dwelling house and other lands specified for £100.

William Dallands delivered to the Mayor and Burgesses four bonds dated 30 April 1569: his bond in £40 for the payment of £25 at Michaelmas; the bond of Dallands and Peter Fary in £40 for payment of £25 at Michaelmas 1570; the bond of Dallands and Fary in £40 for payment of £25 at Michaelmas 1571; finally, the bond of Dallands and Andrew Leake in £40 to pay £25 at Michaelmas 1572. **563**

blank fol. 85r.

2 May 1569 Assembly

John Bell, late Mayor, delivered to the present Mayor, Thomas Doughtie, the copie of a certificate from the Exchequer of the recusancy of the late vicar of Boston for the non-payment of his tenths for the vicarage. fol. 85v. **564**

The Mayor has received the following bonds: for the payment of £17 by William Wesname dated 27 August 1563; for the payment of 26s 8d by Melchior Smyth dated 24 June 1561; for £20 by James Hayward and Robert Pulvertoft to save John Bell harmlesss over the forfeit of a certain keel, dated 17 March 1569; in £10 by William Bonde and Peter Bamforth dated 12 April 1568 to pay the Mayor and Burgesses £6 at Michaelmas 1569; in £10 by the same to pay the (fol. 86r.) Mayor and Burgesses another £6 at Michaelmas 1570; in 60s by William Bonde to pay the Mayor and Burgesses 2d yearly for a house bought by him from the corporation; an acquittance made to the Mayor and Burgesses by the executors of Thomas Browne, esquire, for the payment of £200 in money and plate due by the legacy of Thomas Browne to his son Thomas, dated 16 October 1568; an obligation by Christopher Cowper, John Fox and Richard Cocke to pay £10 to the Mayor and Burgesses, dated 22 October 1565; a bond by which Walter Woodruff is to pay the Mayor and Burgesses 100s dated 23 May 1567. **565**

27 May 1569 Assembly

William Dallands, Christopher Awdley, Andrew Leake and Richard Feilde, of the Common Council did not attend this Assembly though warned "ideo in misericordia quos solvere". **566**

Thomas Doughtie, Mayor, has custody of the following armour: 6 "Alman Revettes" lacking 4 gorgettes, 6 bills, 1 sallett; 3 "sculles"; 3 breasts and 3 backs of "Alman Revettes"; one pair of "vambrasse", one pair of "splentes", one pair of "carses", one pair of "Greves", one pair of gauntlets; 3 "murrans", and 3 "hagabusshes"; 12 swords, 8 daggers, 5 bows and one sheaf of arrows. **567**

568 William Smyth is granted a lease of the profits and revenues of the toll and "Damages Fezaunt" within the borough for a term of 6 years from 1 May last paying a rent of £23 per annum. If William defaults the corporation may re-enter and expel him from the property. Provided that the corporation allows William 20s a year from the rent for the money formerly given him towards his "mayntenaunce of lyvyng".

fol. 87r. Simon Turpyn and Richard Hogekynson are granted a lease of all
569 waifs and strays and the profits of the pounding of the same strays for 6 years from last May Day at a yearly rent of £6 per annum.

570 Whereas Richard Draper, late farmer of the waifs and strays, is content to give up his good will of the same, he is to be granted 40s by the corporation.

571 Memorandum: by an indenture dated 29 April last between John Bell, Mayor, and Thomas Doughtie, Mayor elect, the following were delivered to Thomas: 2 pewter chargers; 3 dozen pewter platters; 12 pewter dishes; 11 banqueting dishes; 15 pewter dishes; 12 platters; 12 dishes; 23 pottingers; 24 saucers; another 18 saucers; 6 wine pots;
fol. 87v. 24 silver spoons, 2 spits; a pair of cobirons; a brasen pot; a "scomer"; a ladle; a "brandreth".

3 June 1569 Assembly

572 John Stamper, one of the Common Council, failed to attend the Assembly.

573 John Bell's account for his mayoralty was examined and he was found to be in debt in the sum of £18 7s 2d, upon "a respectuatur" of £6 13s 4¼d laid out in making the new drain.

574 John Dixon and George Erle were found to be £11 16s 9¾d in arrears on their account for the town's revenues.

575 John Dixon and George Erle were found to be £8 16s 8d in arrears on their account for the erection lands.

7 June 1569 Assembly

576 John Stamper, one of the Common Council, was fined 6s 8d "for certen contemptes and obprobrius ageynst the ordynaunces of the same Borough"; on his promise not to offend again he was returned 4s 8d and the rest was put in the Court Box.

John Margery, one of the Common Council, for procuring suit against Beatrix Hix, widow, out of the court of Boston contrary to the order of the borough, is fined 40s, of which 30s is remitted on his submission to the Mayor and Burgesses. John is to pay the remaining 10s at the next Assembly. fol. 88r. 577

"Item at this Assemble it is agreed that Leonard Irby Squier beyng Deputie Recorder of this Borough and Alderman of the same is licensed by the maior and Burgesses to Absent hymself at his Will and pleasure untill the Fest of all Seyntes next comyng". 578

Likewise William Gannocke, Alderman, is given permission to be absent until Michaelmas next. He is to pay the charges of any messenger sent to notify him of Assembly meetings. 579

William Leyth of Boston, ropemaker and a freeman, contrary to his oath and the laws of the borough has acted by himself and through others to disquiet, trouble, vex and sue divers inhabitants to their great disquiet and cost. He is here dismissed from the freedom and not allowed to trade, unless he submits to the Mayor and Aldermen at the next court on 8 June and promises not to bring such actions against inhabitants of the Borough, except in the town sessions. 580 fol. 88v.

15 July 1569 Assembly

John Dixon, Richard Draper, William Dallands and George Erle, made default for their appearance. 581

John Dixon, one of the Common Council, paid his fine of 12d for his absence in Whitsun week last. 582

John Bell owes upon a "respectuatur" on the foot of his account 49s 10d, which shall be decided at the next Assembly. 583

John Bell made his account for his mayoralty and is in arrears of £13 16s 0¼d, for which he has made a bill to the Mayor and burgesses to be paid at Michaelmas next. 584

7 September 1569

Thomas Doughtie, Mayor, John Bell, John Gawdrye, Anthony Claymonde, Aldermen, Richard Draper, John Lanam, Richard Jefferay and George Erle are to survey Bardike and the lane abutting it against the grounds of William Yaxley and others. They or 4 of them are to certify at the next Assembly how it may be kept sweet and at whose charge. fol. 89r. 585

586 The owners of all goods charged or discharged out of any crayer, ship, or other vessel at the Church staithe and other wharves and staithes, belonging to the borough or other persons, are liable to pay the owners of the wharves and staithes (once in good repair) at a rate to be ordained.

587 William Derby, esquire, and Christopher Awdley did not appear when called.

17 September 1569 Assembly

588 John Margery, John Dixon, Richard Draper, Christopher Awdley, George Erle, Thomas Owresby, and Andrew Leake, of the Common Council, made default at this Assembly when they were called.

589 A "Clowe" is to be made at St John's Bridge at the cost of the borough before 29 September.

fol. 89v. The Bardike shall be scoured and cleaned by all fronting on it from
590 St John's Bridge to a place called Simon Turpyn's corner before 29 September. Also from this corner as far as the "greate pytt" at Wormgate End the Bardike is to be diked at the town's cost, through the grounds of Simon Turpyn, William Hawkrige and Robert Bonner.

591 A "Clowe" is to be made at Wormgate End against the great pit at the town's cost before 29 September. A fine of 3s 4d for every "rode" being unmade.

592 Anthony Claymonde, Alderman, John Lanam, John Wilkynson, and Richard Jefferay are to oversee the making of the "Clowes" and the scouring and cleaning of Bardike from St John's Bridge to Wormgate End.

593 Freemen admitted: [—] Wynterburne of Lincoln, draper, on fine of 100s; Richard Jetter, on fine of 40s.

594 William Leyth is discharged of his freedom and forbidden to occupy any lands or tenements of the Borough after Michaelmas. George Erle, Bailiff, to (?) warn him.

23 September 1569

fol. 90r. Richard Feilde, one of the Common Council, did not attend the
595 Assembly when called.

5 October 1569 Assembly.

The Mayor shall with all expedition demand and collect all the debts and duties owed to the borough. Any refusing to pay shall be sued in the Court of Common Pleas or in the Court of Boston as the Mayor thinks best for the recovery of the debts. **596**

Deeds made by the corporation: indenture dated 18 July 1568 granting to Ralph Spurr the messuage and buildings late Robert Barkar's at the south end of the bridge (on payment of £18 at sealing) for a term of 200 years and an annual payment to the corporation of 2d; bargain and sale dated 1 October 1569 to Alan Manby of a messuage and one rood of land for £15 with an annual rent of 2d and suit of court to the Manor of Halgarth, together with a letter of attorney to George Erle and Andrew Leake; bargain and sale dated fol. 90v. 5 October 1569 to Christopher Cowper of a cottage and garden in Boston for £4 5s; a like deed dated 5 October 1569 to John Barret of a stable on the east part of the water for £4 and a yearly payment of 1d, together with a letter of attorney; indenture dated 1 October 1568 to Thomas Woodruff of Boston granting him a messuage, buildings and garth stede in his tenure on the west side of the water (on payment of £16 by instalments) for a term of 200 years and an annual rent of 1d; bargain and sale dated 5 October 1569 to George fol. 91r. Claymonde of Frampton, gent., of a messuage and [ ] acres of land and pasture in Wiberton, Lincs., late in the tenure of Richard Austen for £61 10s, with a letter of attorney to Andrew Leake and George Erle. **597**

31 October 1569 Assembly

"At this Assemble it is agreed that for asmoche as Thomas Sowthen beyng one of the Aldermen and Justice of the peace within the Borough Doth Willyngly and Wilfully absent hymself att Peterbough and doth not his Dutie and service as a Justice within this Borough ought to doo although he hath ben ofte and many tymes required and desired soo to doo by the mayor and Burgesses of the said Borough, That there shalbe letters directed to hym frome the said Maior and Burgesses to thentente that the same Thomas Sowthen doo personally appere before the said Maior and Burgesses att their Guilde Hall of the said Borough upon thursday Whiche shalbe the tenth day of November next comyng by viijth of the clocke in the firste parte of the same Day not fayling that to doo as he will further answer at his parell for the contrarie". **598**

fol. 91v. Alderman Anthony Claymonde, gent., made his detailed account for
599 the £12 delivered him for the provision of armour lacking in Boston in 1569. He accounted for "suche parcelles of Armor and other necessaries parteynyng to the same" and his expenses about the same in London, as well as payments for the muster day.

600 Agreed that the Borough shall henceforth pay 10s yearly to the Dean and Chapter of Lincoln for the outrent of the parish church of Boston (now belonging to the Mayor and Burgesses but formerly to the priory of St John of Jerusalem in England). The Dean and Chapter remit all arrears due from the borough. [The Latin text of the agreement follows, together with a copy of the award in the Court of Augmentations dated 10 November 1542 of a pension of 10s per annum from the church of Boston to the Dean and Chapter of Lincoln (fols. 92r.–93r.).]

10 November 1569 Assembly

fol. 93v. Thomas Doughtie, the Mayor, delivered into the Treasury of the
601 borough the following bonds: one dated 14 September 1569 by which Alan Manby is bound to pay £6 to the Mayor and Burgesses at Michaelmas 1570; another dated the same day by which the same Manby is to pay a further £6 to the Mayor and Burgesses at Michaelmas 1571; another dated 30 October 1569 by which William Sisterson and others are bound to pay £2 to the Mayor and Burgesses at Michaelmas 1570; another dated the same day by which William Sisterson is bound to pay a further £2 to the Mayor and Burgesses at Christmas 1569; another dated 22 October 1565 by which Christopher Cowper, John Fox, and Richard Cocke are bound to pay £10 to the Mayor and Burgesses at Michaelmas 1569; another dated 22 May
fol. 94r. 1567 by which Thomas Thorye and John Gawdrye are bound to pay £20 to the Mayor and Burgesses at Michaelmas 1568; another dated 23 May 1569 by which Walter Woodruff is bound to pay 100s to the Mayor and Burgesses at Christmas 1569; another dated 30 April 1569 by which William Dallands is bound to pay £25 to the Mayor and Burgesses at Michaelmas 1569.

602 The Mayor and Burgesses delivered to John Bell, late Mayor, an obligation dated 15 March 1568/9, in which James Hayward and Robert Pulvertoft are bound to Bell in £20, "to thentent he may by order Discharge hymself of such sutes as is depending in the Quenes Exchequer at the sute of William leith and to bere his owne charges and take suche advantage of the obligacon as the law will gyff hym".

The Mayor delivered into the Treasury an acquittance dated 12 October 1569 by Lowis Evans,[18] vicar of this borough, acknowledging the receipt of £23 from Thomas Doughtie, Mayor, for all arrears due to Evans for the vicarage. **603** fol. 94v.

Alderman William Derby, esquire, is given licence to be absent until 1 March next, provided he attend the Assembly when warned by the Mayor. **604**

Deeds sealed: one dated 10 November 1569 for the bargain and sale to William Sisterson of one messuage with the buildings of the west part of the haven, late in the occupation of Hercules Lodwicke for £12, plus outrent and suit of court; a letter of attorney dated 31 October 1569 to George Erle and Andrew Leake on behalf of the Mayor and Burgesses to enter all the land and property in the possession of William Leyth belonging to the corporation and to expel him from the same. **605** fol. 95r.

"It is agreed at this assemble that Antony Kyme Gentilman Richard Feilde gent., Jeffrey Ware merchant of the Staple of England and John Margery beyng foure of the nomber of xviij Burgesses shall from hensfurth make their abode and dwellyng Within the this Borough unless they be other wise licenced by the maior and Burgesses for the tyme being". **606**

16 December 1569 Assembly

John Margery paid his 10s fine for contempt at the Assembly on 7 June. **607**

Deeds sealed: a lease for 100 years dated 10 November 1569 to Alexander Skynner, gent., of one rood of land on the west side of the water for 1d a year rent; a release dated 16 December 1569 to Leonard Bowshere, clerk, of his dwelling house. **608**

7 January 1569/70 Assembly

William Dallands, one of the Eighteen, failed to attend, when called. fol. 95v. **609**

17 February 1569/70 Assembly

The Bailiffs are to make an entry into the house purchased from the corporation by Thomas Woodruff (called "loddes howse") for non-payment of the purchase money. **610**

[18] Lowis Evans, vicar, resigned in 1571. LRS 2, p. 311.

611 William Pulvertoft, merchant, is to be admitted a freeman on payment of 40s fine.

24 March 1569/70 Assembly

612 Thomas Sowthen, Alderman and one of the Justices of the Peace, having wilfully absented himself from the borough and not executed his offices, and having failed to return despite warning, is henceforth discharged of his offices.

fol. 96r. Edmund Toynton and Richard Robynson were elected to the
613 Common Council.

614 Jeffrey Ware is discharged from the Common Council for wilfully disobeying the Mayor.

615 John Lanam, one of the Common Council, is elected Alderman; Robert Turpyn is elected in his place on the Common Council.

616 John Bell, Alderman, is elected one of the four Justices of the Peace of the borough.

25 March 1570 Assembly

617 John Bell, Alderman, was sworn as one of the Justices of the Peace; John Lanam was sworn as an Alderman; Edmund Toynton, Richard Robynson and Robert Turpyn were sworn as members of the Common Council.

618 William Derby, Alderman, is elected Mayor for the next year.

fol. 96v. *blank*

5 May 1570: "Assemble of the maior and Aldermen only"

fol. 97r. Sir John David, clerk, parson of North Witham in Kesteven in
619 Lincolnshire paid 10s into the Common Box towards the repair of the bridge and pier at Boston.

19 May 1570 Assembly

620 Richard Draper of Boston is to have a lease from the corporation of "the commoditie and profight of the Fishing to them belongyng Within the haven above the bridge", for ten years, paying 20s per annum; reserving to the Mayor "foure severall Fysshing Dayes at his pleasure", and also reserving to the inhabitants of the borough "Anglyng and bobbyng" during the lease.

Andrew Leake and William Dallands are elected Bailiffs and Collectors of the rents and revenues of the town lands for the next year, being allowed a fee of 53s 4d. fol. 97v. **621**

Lawrence Meres, gent., paid on behalf of Melchior Smyth 14s 4d, part of the 26s 8d owed by Smyth to the corporation by his bill dated 24 June 1569. **622**

Agreed that William Wadesworth and Alderman John Lanam shall pay the £10 for which they are bound, by annual instalments of 40s starting next Lady Day. **623**

William Wadesworth and William Dallandes are to pay 60s they owe the corporation in like fashion, starting with 20s next Lady Day. **624**

23 June 1570 Assembly

Richard Burton, a freeman of Boston, for bringing a legal action against Edmund Jackson, another freeman, without licence of the Mayor, is fined 40s. fol. 98r. **625**

John Carter, a poor man of Boston, is to have the bedemanship that was formerly held by Henry Bell deceased. **626**

The Surveyors of the Highways of the borough are to have timber, stone and lime from the town's store for repairing the new "Clowe" at Hildyke. To be paid for out of the fines levied on common work days. **627**

The Mayor and four Justices are to survey all the houses belonging to the corporation, the bridge and "other necessarie thynges of charges Within this Borough", and determine what repairs need to be done. **628**

An assurance is to be made by the corporation to William Sisterton and his heirs of all the messuages etc. in Boston formerly in the tenure of Robert Dobbes with the Court House adjoining (except the pinfold) on payment of £40. **629**

A lease for 99 years is to be granted to John Lanam of one warehouse and garth stede adjoining to his dwelling house, sometime pertaining to Henry Fox, at a yearly rent of 12d payable at Michaelmas. John Lanam is to pay a fine of £9 for the lease. **630**

Richard Smyth is made a freeman and sworn in; to pay a fine of 20s by annual instalments of 5s. **631**

15 September 1570 Assembly

fol. 99r. Francis Bountyng of Hagworthingham, gent., is admitted and sworn
632 a freeman, paying a fine of 40s.

633 A lease for 23 years to Robert Townley, gent., and his wife Joan, of the Grey Friars in Boston and half an acre of pasture called Castle ground and a little piece of ground on the west part of the Bardike, for a yearly rent of 100s.

634 Robert Bonner did pay to certain inhabitants listed in the Register Book £4 18s 6d, which he received from Thomas Seynt Poll, esquire, for recompense of the lottery money.

22 September 1570 Assembly

635 Robert Turpyn, one of the Common Council, was absent until 9 o'clock.

25 September 1570 Assembly

fol. 99v. The following writings were delivered out of the Treasury to William
636 Derby, Mayor: a bond dated 1 February by which John Lanam is to pay £20 to the corporation; a bill dated 27 August 1563 by which William Wesname, late Alderman, is to pay the corporation £17; a bond of Thomas Dowghtie to pay £4; a bond of William Bonde and Peter Bamforth to pay £6; a bond of Alan Manby to pay £6; a bond of William Dallands to pay £25; a bill of Walter Woodruff to pay £5; a bond of William Sisterson to pay 60s.

fol. 100v. *2 November 1570 Assembly*

637 A lease sealed of the Grey Friars for Robert Townley, gent.

638 Antony Kyme, gent., Richard Feilde and John Margery were absent; order shall be taken because of their continual absences from the Assembly.

639 A letter of attorney sealed for Andrew Leake and William Dallands to take possession of a piece of ground granted to the corporation by Robert Townley, gent.

640 The Mayor and Burgesses are to enter into bonds in £200 to John Browne and Richard Brigges "for the performaunce of a certen arbitrament towching the order and use of Agnes Foxe goods".

641 A letter of attorney sealed for Andrew Leake and William Dallands to take possession from John Browne and Richard Brigges of lands purchased with Agnes Fox's money and by them granted to the corporation.

"Also at the same assemble Leonard Bowsher clerke complaynyng that his wages was to little beyng viij[l] and makyng request that the same myght be amended, ytt was agreed that he shuld have tenne poundes yerely from Mich last and so to contynew". **642**

2 November 1570 Assembly

Agreed that for "the better repair and order of the works above the havyn banks" certain Aldermen be appointed every quarter to survey the same. Mr Gawdrye and Mr Hawkrige are charged with the north part of the banks on the east side of the water; Mr Brigges and Mr Lanam with the south part of the banks on the east side; and Mr Melsonbye and Mr Thorye the banks on the west side. fol. 100v. **643**

Mr Bonner purchased the fee simple of the old school house at Wormgate End and a piece of ground nearby lying within his pasture, he paying £8 when the assurance of the property is sealed. **644**

Lawrence Meres, gent., having asked before to be discharged from his office of Alderman, "for that his business was suche for the service of the Quenes maieste in the North parts as he could not atttend the same", his request was granted. **645**

Antony Kyme, gent., Richard Feilde, gent., and Robert Bonner were in election for the office of Alderman in place of Lawrence Meres; Bonner was chosen. **646**

Alexander Skynner requested the renewal of his lease of 7 acres of pasture on the west side of the water. Agreed to grant him a lease for 11 years from the Purification of Our Lady next, at a yearly rent of 40s. fol. 101r. **646**

10 November 1570 Assembly

Agreed that the yearly rent of the common marsh in the tenure of Thomas Sowthen and William Hawkrige be employed on certain common charges such as "the broviger money for the armtre Fenne" and the like; and the rent be levied from both Sowthen and Hawkrige. **648**

The pit at Bargate end is to be diked and scoured and the cost is to be paid from the fines levied for the common work days. **649**

William Hawkrige, Alderman, is to pay a fine of 40s for "unsemely and undecent words" before the Mayor and his brethren. fol. 101v. **650**

"Certen Juelles in the presse and certen ymplementes" are to be sold at the next Hall to the use of the corporation. **651**

652 The Mayor is to require of Maud Forster a bond to pay £10 to the corporation immediately on her death.

653 Simon Paynter is to have the supervision of the two "Clowes" at the end of Bardike "to take up open and shut as occasion shuld serve for the course of the water to wasshe and scoure Bardike" and to have 10s per annum for his pains.

5 December 1570 Assembly

654 William Porter, gent., was sworn a freeman and assessed to pay [*blank*]

22 December 1570 Assembly

fol. 102r.
655 "At this Assemble it is agreed that Simon Melsonby John Bell and Anthony Cleymond Aldermen Cristopher Awdeley and Richard Jeffrey beyng off the company of the xviij of the common councell with the aide and assistaunce of Mr [*blank*] key clerke beyng the maior chapleyne shall before the next Assemble in the Guildhall view and serche out the povertie Inhabityng within this Borough and the liberties of the same And to make certificate whoo is in povertie and who is able to labor and thentent further orders may be taken for the better releyf of the poore and ympotent and the rest to be put and sett to labor".

19 January 1570/1 Assembly

656 Thomas Derby, merchant of the Staple, and Ralph Pell, draper, were elected to the Common Council in the places of Robert Bonner, now an Alderman, and Richard Robynson, deceased.

657 Agreed that Henry Forest and his wife Rose, executrix of William Wesname, late Mayor, may pay the £17 owed for Wesname's mayoralty on certain agreed days, taking out a bond to pay the same.

658 "Furthermore it is agreed that sute shalbe made to the lord Clynton[19] now Admyrall of Ingland that he with assent and consent of the master Wardans and feliship of Trinite house at Dertford Strond that the maior and Burg' may have the order for the saffe passage of ships to the Borough of Boston in laying of Boys settyng of sea markes in the haven of Boston and the lymittes of the same".

659 Agreed that four dozen leather buckets be purchased for the safeguard of the borough in case of fire.

[19] Edward Fiennes, Lord Clinton, Earl of Lincoln (1512–85), Lord High Admiral.

20 March 1570/1 Assembly

Christopher Hatton[20] and Leonard Irby, esquires, are elected as burgesses for the borough in Parliament, "there to doo all such thynges for and in behalf of the said Borough". **660**

17 March 1570/1 (sic) Assembly

John Skynner, esquire, is ordered to make good his wharf and staithe by Michaelmas next. fol. 103r. **661**

Ralph Pell was sworn as one of the Common Council. **662**

Indenture dated 18 March 1570/1 sealed between the Mayor and Burgesses of Boston and Thomas Quadryng, esquire, Sheriff of the county of Lincoln, for the return of Christopher Hatton, esquire, and Leonard Irby, esquire, as elected Burgesses for the town in Parliament. **663**

A licence granted to Peter Payntre to sell wine according to the statute. fol. 103v. **664**

A lease granted 2 November 1570 by the corporation to Alexander Skynner, esquire, of 7 acres of pasture called Fisshe pasture, lying on the west side of the water between the lands of Francis Robertson to the south and those of William Tupholme's heirs to the north, and abutting on the haven to the east and a common way called the "viij hundredth" to the west. Alexander to have this pasture now in his tenure for 11 years paying 40s per annum. **665**

20 March 1570/1 Assembly

Thomas Derby, merchant of the Staple, was sworn a member of the Common Council. fol. 104r. **666**

Whereas there is a dispute between John Lanam and Robert Wilson (on behalf of Esey Hickes, now Robert's wife, and Agnes Johnson, in the custody of John Lanam) and Richard Brigges and John Browne (executors of Agnes Fox, widow), concerning the bequest of Agnes Fox's implements and household stuff, the question of which goods and chattels are taken in law to be household stuff is to be referred to certain doctors of ecclesiastical law. The parties to stand to such order as the doctors decree, which Leonard Irby, esquire, shall report. **667**

[20] Sir Christopher Hatton (1540–91), later Lord Chancellor; sat as MP for Higham Ferrers 1571, and Northamptonshire 1572.

668 At the special request of Leonard Irby, esquire, it is agreed to reduce the freedom fine assessed on Thomas Wynterburne of Lincoln, draper, from 100s to 66s 8d.

fol. 104v. At the particular request of Kellam Irby, gent., James Worthyngton
669 of London, draper, was admitted a freeeman with a fine of 20s.

25 March 1571 Assembly

670 John Gawdrye, John Lanam and Robert Bonner were put in election for the mayoralty and John Lanam was elected for the next year.

19 April 1571 Assembly

fol. 105r. Thomas Lyfield,[21] esquire, is elected by the whole house to be a
671 co-burgess in Parliament for Boston with Leonard Irby, esquire, in place of Christopher Hatton, esquire, who was elected and now sits for the town of Northampton.

672 The Bailiffs and Collectors of revenues for the borough are to pay 100s to Leonard Irby, esquire, or his deputy for the fee of Edward Fynes, Lord Clinton and Saye, Knight of the Garter and High Admiral of England, as the Steward of the borough of Boston.

fol. 105v. The Bailiffs shall pay Leonard Irby, esquire, £5 in full recompense of
673 his fees and expenses in this present Parliament.

674 "And likewise at this assemble it is agreed that the Bayliffes and collectors of the Rentes revenues and profights of this Borough for the tyme beyng shall from hensfurth yerely content and pay unto George Forster the towne clerke xl^s for his paynes and travail in wrytyng and kepyng of the boke of the lawes and ordynaunces hereaftur to be made and devised in the Guyldehall of this Borough by the maior Aldermen and common councell of this Borough and for the regestryng and writyng of the same in the grate bok of their lawes and ordynaunces to be payd to hym yerely at the feast of Seynt Michell the Archaungell and the Annunciacion of our lady by even portions so long as the same George shall kepe write and reiester the same actes & lawes by the sufferaunce consent and assent of the maior Recorder Aldermen and common councell of this borough".

[21] Thomas Lyfield, MP for Boston 1571; also Surrey 1572, Reigate 1589.

"And whereas the same George Forster before this tyme by the space of thre yeres to be endit at May day next comyng that is to say in the tyme of Mr Bell Mr Doughtie and Mr Derby late maiors of this Borough of Boston has not only kept the said booke of Assemblies but also hath regesterd the same And as unto this tyme the said George hath not been recompensed for the same ytt is therfore agreed at this assemble that the Bailiffes and collectours of the Rentes perteynyng to this Borough shall content and pay to the said George for the said towe last yeres in the tyme of Mr Doughtie and Mr Derby four pounds and for the tyme of Mr Bell x^s only for that leonard Bowsher clerke late Reister of the same assembles had receyved the holl fee of xl^s savyng only the said x^s". **675** fol. 106r.

30 April 1571 Assembly

Christopher Awdley, gent., one of the Common Council, was elected and sworn an alderman in the place of John Lanam who died on 26 April. **676**

William Sisterson was elected and sworn one of the Common Council in place of Christopher Awdley, gent. **677**

John Gawdrye, Alderman, is elected Mayor in the place of John Lanam deceased who died before taking his oath of office. **678**

1 May 1571 Assembly

John Gawdrye took the oath of office as mayor for the next year. **679**

blank fol. 107r.

1 May 1571 [*sic*] *Assembly*

[Repeats entry for Gawdrye taking the oath as mayor.]

Christopher Awdley, gent., Alderman, and Antony Kyme, gent., fol. 108r.
John Wilkynson and Thomas Derby, of the Common Council, failed to attend. **680**

7 June 1571 Assembly

The Surveyors of the Highways in the borough shall spend such money as convenient, by the advice of the Mayor and Aldermen, for making one "clowe" on the west part of Cow Bridge so water may come through the New Dike to the hospital end and for scouring, cleansing and repairing the same dike. The money to be levied from persons assessed according to the statute. **681**

fol. 108v. 682 There was delivered to John Gawdrye, Mayor, the following bonds owed to Agnes Fox, widow, deceased: one by John Richardson of Coningsby to pay £18; another by Richard Fissher of [—] to pay 26s 8d; another by Robert Pails of [—] to pay £10; another by Nicholas Fox to pay £20; another by John Barret to pay 26s 8d; two by Peter Symson of Lincoln to pay £4; one privy seal for £25. Sum of all the debts owing her: £69 13s 4d.

683 The following bonds due to the mayor and burgesses were also delivered to the mayor: one by William Derby, esquire, late mayor, to pay £133 0s 10d; another by John Lanam and Andrew Leake to pay £10; another by George Claymonde, John Hiltoft and Anthony Claymonde, gentlemen, to pay £20.

fol. 109r. **684** Agreed that Andrew Leake of the Common Council shall be Bailiff of the Erection Lands and also of the lands given by Henry Fox, late Alderman, for providing a priest to attend the Mayor, and also of the lands purchased according to the will of Agnes Fox, widow. He is to make his account and have 26s 8d yearly.

685 Likewise William Dallands shall be Bailiff of all the Corporation manors and lands. He is to make his account yearly and have 53s 4d for his pains.

686 William Derby, esquire, late Mayor, is given leave to be absent until Michaelmas next, but to attend the Assembly days when notified.

8 June 1571 Assembly

fol. 109v. **687** Lease of 21 years granted to William Leyth of the messuage where he now dwells and 7 acres of pasture, and of the messuage at Wormgate called "Wayne house" and 7 acres of pasture, at an annual rent of
fol. 110r. £6 13s 4d.

688 Three bonds due to the Mayor and Burgesses were delivered to Mr Gawdrye, mayor: one by William Wadesworth and John Lanam dated 7 March 1565/6 to pay £10 at Michaelmas 1569; another by Alan Manby, Richard Baxter, and William Whithede dated 14 September 1569 to pay £6 at Michaelmas 1571; another by William Dallands and Peter Payntre dated 30 April 1569 to pay £25 at Michaelmas 1571.

5 July 1571 Assembly
"Att this assemble Henry Holland[22] clerk Bacheler in Divinitie is elected named and appoynted to be vicar of the parishe Church of this Borough upon condicon that he kepe his reisidence in and upon the same unlesse he have som reasonable cause to the contrarie". **689**

9 August 1571 Assembly fol. 110v.
Alderman John Bell failed to attend, though notified. **690**

Agreed to demand a relief of Mr Holland for his lands in Swineshead and to seize two "wardes" there. **691**

William Dallands and Andrew Leake, Bailiffs of the borough, are authorised to make a re-entry in Thomas Wryght's dwelling house for non-payment of £15 owed for the purchase of the house. **692**

William Yaxley, gentleman, agreed to pay [*blank*] to the corporation for such fines due for his non-appearance in King's Bench according to a writ of attaint between Henry Aiscough, esquire, plaintiff, and Robert Mounson, esquire, and others, defendants. Yaxley paid 40s to the Mayor and the rest was remitted. **693**

Agreed to grant to William Yaxley, gentleman, a lease for 21 years of 4 acres of pasture and one acre of arable land in Skirbeck for a yearly rent of 35s and a fine of £7 at next Lady Day. **694** fol. 111r.

Agreed to grant John Stamper a lease for 21 years of 3 roods of pasture in Skirbeck for an annual rent of 5s, together with a fine of 30s, of which he paid 10s now and the rest to be paid next Lady Day. **695**

Andrew Taylour, beer brewer, is to pay 60s at Christmas next in full payment of all debts owed by him to the corporation. **696**

3 September 1571 Assembly
Anthony Kyme, gentleman, and Andrew Leake, of the Common Council, failed to attend, though summoned. **697**

John Gawdrye, Mayor, Leonard Irby, esquire, Simon Melsonbye, John Bell, Richard Brigges, Anthony Claymonde, William Hawkrige and Robert Bonner, Alderman, on behalf of the borough have purchased for 200 marks from Sir Henry Clinton, knight, all the wood and underwood growing in 20 acres of Fulletby Wood in the parish of [*blank*]. The Mayor and Burgesses to assign and sell the same wood for the profit of the Borough. Approved by the Assembly. fol. 111v. **698**

[22] Henry Holland B.D., vicar 1571–84.

699 Agreed that Andrew Leake, John Stamper, Edmund Jacson, Roger Browne, Elizabeth Dixon, widow, Beatrix Hix, widow, Francis Hood and John Wood "may sell countrey ale and bere within their howses only and not to utter or sell any countrey Ale or bere furthe of their howses upon payne of every Default iij^{s} iiij^{d}."

fol. 112r.
700 John Bell, Anthony Claymonde, Thomas Thorye, Thomas Doughtie, Aldermen, and Thomas Owresby of the Common Council, are to view and lay out the 20 acres of wood bought from Sir Henry Clinton according to the bargain and agreement with him.

701 Those licensed as tipplers in the borough whose names follow [*blank*] may sell country ale and beer "aswell in their houses as also out of their houses".

8 September 1571 Assembly

702 William Hawkrige, Robert Bonner, Aldermen, Thomas Owresby, George Erle, Richard Jefferay and Robert Turpyn, of the Common Council, and John Stamper, John Wilkynson, Richard Hix, John Alderchurche, Ralph Pell, and Thomas Tymson, constables, are to rate and assess every man in this borough for the taxes granted by Parliament on 2 April 1571.

28 September 1571 Assembly

fol. 112v.
703 John Bell, Anthony Claymonde, Thomas Thorye, and Thomas Doughtie, Aldermen, by the agreement of William Hawkrige and others previously appointed for the assessment of the tax, are authorised to rate and assess the inhabitants and certify the alteration of the first view and assessment to the Mayor and Burgesses before 8 October next.

704 One bond dated 10 October 1570 was delivered out of the Treasury to Mr Gawdrye, Mayor, whereby John Browne, gentleman, is to pay £30 to the corporation at Michaelmas 1571.

17 October 1571 Assembly

705 Whereas the Queen by her privy seal has discharged the borough of Boston of the tax granted by her last Parliament in April, for the cost of obtaining this every man assessed for the tax shall pay at the rate of 3s 4d per £1 or 2d per shilling.

7 September [*sic*] *1571 Assembly*

John Gawdrye, Mayor, is to be granted a lease for 21 years of the Wayne house and 14 acres of land lately held by William Leythe, at an annual rent of £6 16s. Also Mr Gawdrye is to enquire of Mr Reede of Wrangle by what title he detains certain land in [*blank*] belonging to the corporation, and whether he will allow the corporation to enjoy the same and pay his arrrears for it; to make entry and commence a suit for recovery if he refuses. fol. 113r. **706**

9 November 1572 [*sic*] *Assembly*

Richard Draper, George Erle and John Wilkynson, of the Common Council, failed to attend. **707**

Agreed that the Mayor should come to an agreement with Mr Laurence Meres, gentleman, concerning the redemption and discharge of his patent and annuity of 40s. fol. 113v. **708**

The following "sessors for the payment of the Quenes majesties provision"[23] were appointed: Anthony Claymonde, Robert Bonner, Aldermen, Thomas Owresby, Richard Draper, Robert Turpyn and William Sisterson for the east side of the water; Philip Curtes, Richard Feilde, Ralph Pell and John Stather for the west side. **709**

Agreed that Mr [*blank*] take 4 or 6 of the Aldermen and Common Council to view St John's church and decide what repairs are needed. **710**

"Also at this assemble the company of Taylors upon complaynt were warned to appere befor the Maior and Burgesses in the Guildhall and there it was agreed by common assent that when any of this Borough shall nede a Taylour to work in his house That then upon desire made to the wardens of the company or to one of them the same wardens or one of them . . . shall appoynt one sufficient workman to worke with hym or them from tyme to tyme as shall nede to have such a workman". **711**

"Also at this assemble it is agreed that the sute for their licence to transport vi thowsand quarters of grane and Corne And A thowsand poundes of money to be opteyned at the Quenes Maiesties hands to be repaid ageyne to her Grace in vj yeres shall go forward and to be put in sute". **712**

[23] Purveyance was a tax levied for the maintenance of the royal household.

16 November 1571 Assembly

fol. 114r.

713 "At this assemble it is agreed that the names of all suche persons as be wilfull and obstinate in gevyng ther charitie toward the releif of the poore in Boston shalbe certefied to the Bysshop or to his ordinarie of the Diocese of lincoln declaryng their untowardnes in the same to thentent further order may be taken with them accordyng to the statute in that case provided".[24]

714 "Also where there is demaunded of Mr [*blank*] key clerk beyng Chaplen to the maior of this Borough for the tyme beyng commonly called the maior chapleyn A subsidie for his stipende whyche he hath of the maior and Burgesses by reason of the gifte of one henry Foxe late one of the Aldermen of this Borough it is agreed that the payment thereof shalbe stayed and not payd untill suche tyme as the same maior and Burgesses may be fully certified whether the said stipend is charged to the said subsidie or no".

17 December 1571 Assembly

715 The following letter, read in the Assembly, is to be sent to Christopher Awdley, gentleman, in London

"Mr Audeley I have now redde your sundry letters perceyvyng therby our former letters commen to your handes and howe fare you have proceded therein concernyng our sutes as also remembryng us of the office of the Admyraltie within our liberties and what privilege and

fol. 114v.

commoditie myght growe unto us by the same (as sundry other portes have the like Whyche as you thinke wold nowe be opteyned for the valeue of one C^{li} and under the colour thereof in renuyng of our charter and enlargement of the same our liberties whiche may be amended where upon havyng hadd some consideracon with the advice conference of the holl howse we finde the same nolesse necessarie mete and convenyent for us then alredy you have considered And if the state of our towne and port whereof suche as thos townes you write of and others wold be no small commoditie as ease to us and our Inhabitauntes But beyng as we are and as you know fallen in suche decay and so destitute of shippes and trade of Shippyng as first without som provision and meane to helpe and better furnysshe the same Will that Office neyther gretely be commodious for us nor yet our Towne contynue long without hasard of utter ruyne and dekay whiche to our powers we wold be glad to helpe And by godds grace doo intend to bend ourselfes to the redresse thereof And for that we wold be loythe to sett the Cart afore the horsse to goo about to

[24] Under Acts of 1552 and 1563 persons refusing to pay poor relief could be referred to the local bishop for admonition.

purchase hawkes raither occasion to sell beyng charged to pay Sir henry Clynton CC marks for certen woodes and tymber provided for the repayre of our Stathes and havyn bankes the employment whereof and other charges about the said wilnot coste A little As also this next yere muste be payd to Mastres Browne CC^{li} whiche must be payd and provided for Wherfore we shall hertely require you to have consideracon and to use your discrecion in our sutes towchyng our twoo former requestes Whiche if we may opteyne wold be so commodious unto us as we hope will therby to helpe us and furnysshe a greate part fol. 115r. of our wantes but sure except we can first fynde some meanes for the releif of our dekay by gettyng som thyng whiche we cannot devise by any better meanes then these twoo we have alredy taken in hand in hope well to opteyne the same though our friendship suche in Courte whiche faylyng is now at this pynche we are utterly in disspare to attemptt any further/ And then to seke that Office to our charge and as neyther in case or Abilitie to take commoditie therby And to disburse money for the same whiche we have not were some folie And as we can gether by your last letter the reversion of the office off the Steuardship of our Towne upon this talke you have hadd is sought for our libertie wherein we wolde be loithe to lose in sellyng the other to our charge/ But once ageyne for our sutes whereof we percyve the licence will not be moche sticked at And if the other will not be hadd yet goo Forwhard with that/ But some diligence must be used to have it in tyme and with spede before the sprynge of the yere/ or elles small good wilbe doon therby bothe our sutes opteyned and this we are moost willyng to goo forward with the Office of the Admyraltie/ And upon intellegence from you of the same we will giff you further instructions therein and send you up a Draught of the same all redy drawen Whiche shuld have past long sence And thus havyng uttered unto you our myndes at large we refer the rest to your good discrecion and faithfull intent as knoweth the lord whoo prosper you in all your affares and sutes".

Copy of Lord Burghley's letter: **716**
"Aftur my hertie Commendacions/ Where the Office off Recorder of that your towne of Boston hath ben long synce geven unto me by fol. 115v. patent/ the exercise whereof I have used as I may to commyt unto you A Deputie forasmoche as my late Deputie therein master leonard Irby is departed this present liff I beyng carefull to substitute such A one in the place as for honestie and lernyng were sufficient and fitt I have thought to recommend unto you and by thes my letters doo nominate appoynt and substitute as my Deputie Recorder of the said Towne of Boston my verey lovyng frende Mr Stephyn Thymolby A gentilman approved honestie verey well lerned in the lawes of the

Realme and your neighbor praying and requiryng you so to accepte hym and to yelde unto hym the reputacon and goodwill that the place requireth and is Dewe to his honestie and lernyng whereof nothyng doubtyng but you shall have good prooffe to your contentacon I byd you hertely fare well from Grenewiche the last day of November 1571.

Your very lovyng frend Burley".

717 Copy of Sir Henry Clinton's letter:

"Where as the Office of the Stuardship of your Towne of Boston hath ben long synce geven unto my lord my fader whoo heretofore hath bestowed the same Office upon me with the fee thereunto belongyng have care aftur the deathe of Mr leonard Irby in makyng of my choyse of A fit man whoo shuld or wold be bothe able with lernyng with honestie to discharge the same/ have and doo by thes my letters recommend/ nominate appoynt and substitute for the exersysyng of the same Office of the Said Stuardship my lovyng frende Mr Stephyn Thymolby prayng you so to accepte and allow of hym And further
fol. 116r. doo by these my letters graunte and auctorize the said Stephyn Thymolby to take and receyve the fee dewe and belongyng to the said office and for the excercisyng of the same And these my letters With an acquitaunce of his hand for the receyte of the same shalbe your discharge aswell ageynst my lord my fader or ageynst me And thus I commyt you to god from london the Second of December 1571

Your lovyng frend H Clynton[25]

To my verie lovenge frendes the Maior Burgeses & Commynaltie of the towne of Boston".

20 December 1571 Assembly

718 Anthony Kyme, gentleman, Richard Feilde, and John Fox stood for election to the place of Alderman left vacant by the death in London on 3 November of Leonard Irby, esquire. Anthony Kyme was elected.

719 Simon Turpyn, John Harcastell and Henry Parker stood for election to the Common Council in place of Anthony Kyme. Simon Turpyn was elected.

[25] Sir Henry Clinton (d. 1616), son of Edward, Lord Clinton, sat as MP for Lincolnshire 1571.

31 January 1571/2 Assembly

"Att this assemble it is agreed that Cristofer Audeley gent shall not procede any further in the sute for the office of the Admyraltie unlesse the maior and Burg. and their Successors may have good assuraunce from the Quenes maiestie her heires and successours and with all comodities and profights that may arise and growe within the libertie of Boston or in any otherwise perteyning to the same office within the same libertie and without paying of any yerely Rent for the same (except it may be reasonably rated) And likewise that no other office for that purpose but suche as the maior and Burgesses and their Successours shall appoynt to the same from tyme to tyme And furthermore unlesse licence and sufficient Warrant may be hadd in the former sute to cary A certen nomber of grane accordyng to suche former letters as hath ben sente to the said Mr Awdeley". fol. 116v. **720**

Since the mayor's chaplain Mr [*blank*] Key has been instituted to the rectory of Gayton le Marsh, Lincolnshire, and cannot hold the two offices together, it is agreed that he shall relinquish his office of chaplain and will receive no more wages after Lady Day. **721**

29 February 1571/2 Assembly

Henry Marten paid 3s 4d of his freedom fine of 10s and the remainder was remitted because he is poor. fol. 117r. **722**

Simon Turpyn took his oath as one of the Common Council. **723**

Before [*dates blank*] the Mayor and Burgesses are to make an assurance of the custody, wardship and marriage of [*blank*] to Alderman Thomas Doughtie who is to pay 40s at the next Assembly after the assizes in Lincoln. **724**

Francis Fountayne, gent., is to have two ash trees growing at the Tower in Boston for 22s, as assessed by the Mayor and certain Aldermen. **725**

25 March 1572 Assembly

Simon Melsonbye, William Hawkrige, Richard Brigges, Anthony Claymonde, Robert Bonner, Christopher Awdley, and Anthony Kyme, Aldermen, were put in election for the mayoralty: of these Brigges, Bonner and Kyme stood for election and Robert Brigges was chosen Mayor by "free elleccion particularly Aswell of the maior and Aldermen As also of the Common Councell". fol. 117v. **726**

Stephen Thymolby, esquire, was admitted and sworn a freeman and then sworn as Deputy Recorder of the borough under Sir William Cecil, knight, Lord Burghley, chief Recorder. **727**

728 John Margery, one of the Common Council, made default of his attendance.

9 April 1572 Assembly

fol. 118r. "At this assemble it is agreed that where as the Lord Admyrall hath
729 directed his letters unto the Maior and Burgesses of this Borough to have the nominacon and appoyntment of the Burgesses of the same Borough for the parlyament whiche shall begyn at Westminster the viijth day of May next ensuyng, That he the same Lord Admyrall shall appoynt and name one of the same Burgesses upon conditon that he the same Burgesse so beyng elect and named by the said Lord Admyrall shall discharge the said Maior and Burgesses of suche costes and charges as shalbe dewe to hymn for his said Burgesship duryng and for all such tyme as the parliament shall contynue and endure".

18 April 1572 Assembly

730 Stephen Thymolby, esquire, Deputy Recorder, William Derby, esquire, Christopher Awdley and Anthony Kyme, gentlemen, Aldermen, are authorised to make suit unto the Lord Admiral, Lord
fol. 118v. Burghley and others of the Privy Council to obtain a licence to buy and export 10,000 quarters of corn and grain. They are also to try to obtain for the corporation the whole authority and jurisdiction of the Admiralty within the borough.

731 Sir William Harryson, clerk, Vicar of Kirton in Holland, is appointed the Mayor's chaplain, with the wages etc. specified in the will of Agnes Fox, widow, and as enjoyed by Sir Key, clerk, the late chaplain.

732 Stephen Thymolby, esquire, Deputy Recorder, and William Dod-
fol. 119r. dynton, esquire, were elected the borough's two Burgesses in the Parliament meeting at Westminster on 8 May next "without fees or wages".

29 April 1572 Assembly

733 George Forster, Town Clerk, delivered to the town Treasury four bonds of Robert Wayde and others for the performance of the office of keeper of the Queen's gaol, saving the borough harmless against any
fol. 119v. escapes: one by Robert Wayde, Thomas Wryght and George Hassell in £50 dated 17 March 1570/1; another by Robert Wayde and Robert Bryan in £10 dated 31 March 1571; another by Robert Wayde and William Holden of Butterwick in 100s dated 31 March 1571; another by Robert Wayde and Thomas Shotilwod in 100s dated 31 March 1571.

John Margery, William Dallands, John Stamper, Philip Curtes, Richard Feilde and Simon Turpyn, of the Common Council, failed to attend contrary to order. **734**

Stephen Thymolby, esquire, Deputy Recorder, and Christopher Awdley, gent., Alderman, are authorised to make suit unto the Lord Admiral, Lord Burghley and other members of the Queen's Council to get a licence to buy and transport overseas 10,000 quarters of corn and grain. And also to make suit to obtain the Admiralty jurisdiction within the borough of Boston as well as the "government of the Bekonship Within the port and haven". **735** fol. 120r.

End of the statutes and orders made in the time of John Gawdrye, Mayor of Boston, 1572. **736**

blank fol. 120v.

1 May 1572 Assembly

Richard Brigges, Alderman, having been elected last Lady Day, took the oath of Mayor, Escheator and Clerk of the Market. fol. 121r. **737**

22 May 1572 Assembly

Simon Turpyn requests to be discharged from the office of farmer of the waifs and strays and of "the faldage and pynnyng" within the borough. It is agreed that he may be discharged on condition that he pays £4 to the corporation on 30 September next, which Simon and his brother Robert Turpyn have promised to do. **738**

It is also agreed that as Simon Turpyn is discharged from the farm of waifs, strays and poundage for which he paid £6 per year, the farm shall be let to Richard Draper, farmer of the parsonage, for £4 a year from May Day last until the expiry of his lease of the parsonage. The corporation have the right of re-entry if the rent is not paid within 12 days of the due date. With the proviso that before 20 June Draper shall, at the charge of the corporation, make a new fold on the west part of the water to impound all strays taken in that area. **739** fol. 122r.

William Wadesworth, late of Boston, draper, on 13 May 1572 brought into the port of Boston 2 tuns of Gascon wine from France on a ship called the Grace of God of Kirkaldy in Scotland, of which one William Key, a Scotsman, is master and owner and not one of the Queen's subjects, contrary to statute. Whereupon Roger Cockes of Boston, yeoman, exhibited a bill of information to the Mayor and Justices of the Peace on 14 May claiming the wine should be forfeit, **740** one moiety to the Queen, the other to him. Nevertheless "for asmuch as the same William Waddesworth is a verey poore man and in great dette", the Mayor and Burgesses remit the forfeiture of the wine.

17 June 1572 Assembly

741 Agreed tht "no person nor Inhabitaunte of this Borough shall from hensfurth utter or sell by retayle any ale or bere brued out of this Borough", except those hereafter named: William Dallands, Andrew Leake, John Stamper, Beatrix Hix, widow, Ralph Pell, Margaret Browne, widow, John Ward, Francis Hoode; offenders pay 3s 4d fine.

742 Also agreed that "none Inhabitauntes within this Borough shall from
fol. 123r. hensfurth utter or sell any ale by retayle aither in his howse or out of his howse brued out of this Borough", except those hereafter named: Thomas Gooddyng, William Adams, Jennett Cartwryght, widow, Robert Burnes, Roger Browne, Richard Kelsey, Ralph Spurr, Richard Forster; upon pain of 3s 4d fine.

743 For the better execution of these orders Thomas Wymbische, gentleman, shall view and search what ale and beer brewed outside the borough is brought here and who sells it in or out of their houses. And for his work he shall take 1d for every such kilderkin of ale and beer and 1d for every dozen gallons of ale, accounting to the Mayor weekly for the same. Half the money shall be for the use of the corporation in repairing and making of staithes, and the other half shall go to Wymbische. Provided that no money be levied on beer or ale brewed out of the borough which is bought by inhabitants for their household consumption.

25 July 1572 Assembly

fol. 123v. Thomas Doughtie and Anthony Kyme, gentlemen, two of the
744 Aldermen, failed to attend the Mayor at the proclamation of the fair and the holding of the Piepowder Court.

29 July 1572 Assembly

745 John Matson of Boston, "clothe dryver" was admitted and sworn a freeman, paying a fine of 20s.

746 Conveyance in fee simple made to Richard Childe of Boston (in consideration of £28 10s) of the messuage etc. where Richard now
fol. 124r. dwells. He has paid 10s now and the remaining £28 will be paid when the deeds are sealed and delivered. He is to pay 2d yearly and make suit of court at the leets held at Michaelmas and Easter.

18 August 1572 Assembly

It is agreed to pay a yearly rent of 40s to Richard Marley, Bailiff to Robert Dymock, esquire, on the manor of Armtree in Wildmore in the parish of Coningsby, Lincolnshire, for the lease of the ferry which he lately bought from Cuthbert Bothe. **747**

25 August 1572 Assembly

Leases etc. sealed: one to Richard Childe for a house and garden at fol. 124v. the Bridge foot on the west side of the water, for 1000 years paying 2d **748** a year; another to John Gawdrye, Alderman, of the "Waywen house" and 7 acres of pasture and arable given by Agnes Fox to the use of 4 Bedesmen, paying £3 4s 8d a year, 3 acres of the Erection lands, for 13s 4d a year, and 4 acres of pasture belonging to the corporation, for 13s 4d a year, all for 21 years; a letter of attorney to Leonard Butcher [sic] to take possession of two tenements and a garth stede to the use of the corporation according to the deed of Simon Mason dated 14 June 1571; a lease to Ralph Poulle for 21 years of 2 tenements at Bar Bridge for 40s a year; another to George Erle of a stable, warehouse and garth stede in Cocklers lane for 300 years, paying 4d a year; an indenture to Richard Marley for the yearly payment of 40s for Langrick ferry.

Richard Childe paid £24 for the purchase of his house in Boston. Mr **749** Mayor received 13s 8d out of the sealing box and 51s 9d out of the fol. 125r. Court box.

William Sisterson of the Common Council at this assembly gave to the corporation a double lock with two keys for the chest where the common seal is kept. **750**

William Dallands is chosen Bailiff of the Corporation lands and allowed £4 a year for his collection. **751**

John Fox having expended 52s 4d on the repair of "cooy pitt" long ago, he shall be paid 50s in equal parts at Michaelmas and Lady Day. **752**

19 September 1572 Assembly

Edmund Borough, late apprentice to Margery Hallywell, was admitted and sworn a freeman, paying a fine of 3s 4d. **753**

3 October 1572 Assembly

Agreed that a letter of attorney be made and sealed to William Dallands fol. 125v. and Andrew Leake, Bailiffs of the Corporation lands, for them to make **754** entry into any lands unlawfully detained from the borough and to distrain any person not paying their due rents to the borough.

8 December 1572 Assembly

755 William Sisterson agrees to keep to the agreement made between him and the corporation concerning the purchase of the late house and court house formerly held by Robert Dobbes deceased. Since the banks and staithes of the houses are in great ruin and decay, the corporation grants a lease to William for 20 years of 4 acres of pasture

fol. 126r. at Budgate, at an annual rent of 23s 4d.

756 Simon Turpyn paid to the Mayor £4 in full discharge of all rent owed by him for the farm of the toll and poundage, formerly granted to him.

19 December 1572 Assembly

757 A lease dated 10 August 1572 sealed for Robert Bonner of Boston, merchant, of a messuage called "the Scole howse" at Wormgate End. The lease to be for 99 years successively in a perpetual fee farm for an annual rent of 1d payable at Michaelmas.

758 A lease dated 8 December 1572 sealed for Philip Curtes of a garden lately John Huntwike's on the west part of the water between the garden stede late Peter Payntre's and now John Goldesborough's on the south, and the highway on the north, abutting the lands of William Sisterson (late Robert Dobbes') on the west. The lease to be for 1,000 years with an annual rent of 1d, Curtes having paid £4 to the corporation.

759 John Bell and William Gannocke, Aldermen, and Andrew Leake and Robert Turpyn of the Common Council failed to attend this Assembly.

29 January 1572/3 Assembly

fol. 127r. John Stamper paid to Richard Brigges, Mayor, 20s in full payment of

760 30s for a fine for a lease of 3 roods of pasture.

13 February 1572/3 Assembly

761 The four keys to the Treasury chest where the common seal is kept were delivered, one each to Richard Brigges, Mayor, Simon Melsonbye, Alderman, John Gawdrye, Alderman, and John Fox of the Common Council.

762 It was agreed to grant to John Fox, one of the Common Council, a lease for 21 years of two acres of arable land in Boston field now occupied by him for a yearly rent of 6s.

9 March 1572/3 Assembly
Agreed to make a grant to John Wilkynson of a stable and tenement in Bocher Row, lately occupied by William Wadesworth, for a fine of £7 and an annual rent of 1d together with suit of court at the Great Leet of the Manor of Hallgarth. fol. 127v. **763**

764 "Also at this assemble it is agreed that no maner of person or persons Inhabityng or dwellyng within this Borough or the liberties of the same shall from hencefurth kepe any greate dogg cald mastiffs or grounde hounde spanyell or other dogg within his or their howse or howses except they do kepe them tyed up in the night tyme and other tymes as the case and nede shall require unlesse suche person and persons so kepyng any suche dogg or dogges be or is rated taxed and sessed to pay subsidy to the Quenes maiestie".

25 March 1573 Assembly
Simon Melsonbye, William Hawkrige, Anthony Claymonde, Thomas Thorye, Robert Bonner, Christopher Awdley and Anthony Kyme, Aldermen, were put in election for the mayoralty. Simon Melsonbye, Robert Bonner and Anthony Kyme were put in "the second eleccion" and Bonner was chosen Mayor. fol. 128r. **765**

27 March 1573 Assembly
766 "Att this Assemble it is agreed that Anthony Cleymond & Cristofer Awdeley two of the Aldermen and Richard Draper William Dalland and Thomas Oresby thre of the xviii of the common councell of this Borough shall viewe and provide certen howses for the placyng of Straungers".

767 William Derby, esquire, Simon Melsonbye, John Gawdrye, William Gannocke, Robert Bonner, and Christopher Awdley, Aldermen, or most of them, have power to grant licenses for the purchase and transport abroad of grain (except wheat), provided that the Mayor always be one of them.

fol. 128v. **768** "Also where as Edward Astell of Boston musicion with his servauntes and apprentizes be appoynte to be the waytes of this Borough And to play every mornyng throwe out the Borough from Michaelmas untill Cristymmas and from the xiith day until Ester (Sondayes holydayes and Fridayes except) unlesse som cause reasonable may be to the contrarie ytt is therfore agreed at this assemble that for and toward their paynes and travell in this behalf every Alderman to pay unto the said Edward yerely so long as he shall contynue and be wayte of this Borough iiij^{s} at Cristymas & Ester by evyn porcions and every one of the xviij Burg to pay yerely ii^{s} at the dayes and tymes by evyn porcions and every other Inhabitaunte and dweller within this Borough to pay yerely to the same Edward at like dayes by evyn porcions all such somme and sommes of money as shall from tyme to tyme be rated taxed and sessed severally upon every of them by the maior Recorder and Aldermen of the same Borough".

769 At the request of certain glovers of the borough William Derby, esquire, Simon Melsonbye, Anthony Claymonde and Christopher Awdley, gentlemen, Aldermen, shall prepare draft orders and constitutions for the better government of that trade.

fol. 129r.
770 Robert Wayde, Gaoler and keeper of the Queen's prison in Boston, has promised the corporation that he will at his own charge supervise and clean all the armour, harness and artillery of the town. For this he has been discharged of the 5 marks he owed for the rent of his house last Lady Day. Also the corporation will pay him 40s yearly and provide him with a livery gown such as the Serjeants at Mace wear. He is to attend the Mayor at the mayoral election, when the new Mayor takes his oath, at all fairs and markets, sessions of the peace, leets, lawdays and whenever the Mayor commands him. He is to be given a "chawder" of lime to mend his house called the gaoler's house.

30 March 1573 Assembly

fol. 129v.
771 Richard Hogekynson was admitted and sworn a freeman, 6s 8d of the fine of 20s being remitted for his past service in certain offices for the borough.

772 Indenture dated 20 August 1572 sealed and delivered, by which the corporation grants to Thomas Doughtie, gentleman, a lease for 40 years of a messuage, buildings and 5 acres of pasture on the west side of the water in Boston, lately inhabited by Simon Turpyn and Isabel his wife (formerly married to Thomas Deyne of Boston, deceased), for a rent of £4 6s 8d per annum. On condition that the corporation have power to distrain or re-enter on non-payment of rent, and also have power to remove any trees and stones on the premises. Doughtie within five years is to plant one hundred trees or sets of ash or elm and preserve them from damage and he must not let the other part of the Friars called "fyve acres" without the wall to any other than his
fol. 130v. family without licence of the corporation; he may however remove the horse mill on the premises.

Another indenture dated 20 February 1572/3 was sealed and delivered to Robert Byrde alias Cooke by which the corporation grants Byrde a lease for 21 years of a messuage against the Corn Market on the east side of the water, between the highway to south and east, Richard Brigges, Alderman, to the north and Robert Browne to the west. Byrde to pay 20s rent per annum and leave "untaken away all sealynges wyndowes glasse portalles dorres threswoldes and lockes with the keyes belongyng". The corporation have rights of distraint and re-entry on non-payment of rent. **773** fol. 131r.

On payment of £30 a bargain and sale dated 20 March 1572/3 was made by the corporation to John Slater of Boston of a messuage in Boston called "Trinite hall" with a little garden and the moiety of a lane lying on the north part of the garden in the tenure of John on the east side of the water in a place called Wormgate. To hold of the corporation as of the manor of Halgarth in socage with a rent of 2d a year, together with suit of court at the two great leets of the corporation. William Dallands and Andrew Leake were authorised by letter of attorney to deliver seisin of the premises to John Slater. **774** fol. 131v.

At this Assembly with the consent of the Mayor, Aldermen and Common Council, John Slater, John Curtes and Robert Stevynson were appointed Collectors for the relief of the poor[26] until the feast of St Batholomew next. **775**

Likewise Anthony Claymonde, gent., one of the Aldermen, and George Erle, one of the Common Council, were appointed Supervisors of the poor for the same term. **776**

20 April 1573 Assembly

Whereas John Coffey, one of the Serjeants of the corporation, died on 16 April 1573, Richard Turner, son of Edmund Turner, late Alderman, is chosen in his place. Richard Turner, together with Richard Jefferay and William Sisterson, is to give bond in £200 for the due execution of the office. **777** fol. 132r.

Agreed that every freeman of the borough who shall sell or transport any corn beyond the seas in any foreign ship or bottom shall pay 12d per 20 quarters in toll. **778**

[26] The appointment of collectors for the poor was authorised by law in 1563; overseers in 1572.

fol. 132v. 779 Any freeman shipping any grain or wine in any ship being his own goods shall be discharged of paying any tolls.

780 Any stranger shipping any corn out of the port of the borough shall pay 2d for every quarter of corn in toll.

23 April 1573 Assembly

781 Ralph Pell and Thomas Derby, of the Common Council, neglected to attend, though warned.

fol. 133r. *blank*

fol. 133v. 782 "I commend me unto yowe, Where of late I was a meanes unto the Quenes Maiestie for the bennefit of your Towne that yow mighte have lycens to transport thereby a certayne quantite of corne I am given to understand and yt partly apperithe that your ymmoderate use of the said Lycens haithe caused the prices of grayne rounde aboute yowe to increase in suche sorte as upon certificate of the said increase and the dearthe that is Lyke to ensue I have bene necessarily moved to derecte my Lettres to all the portes within that countie for the Restrayninge of transportacion of all manner of grayne untill furder order shalbe by me given therin Lyke as I have also done in other Countries upon the Lyke certificates The coppye of which my Letteres shalbe deliverde unto yow These are particulerly to requier yow not only to obey the contentes of the said Lettres of Restrainte butt also hereafter when the cause of the Restraint shall cease to use more discretion and moderacion in your Lycens to the ende yow maye enioye the same and I have no cause to repente the procuringe you of So fare yowe well frome Westminster the seconde of Maye 1573.

Your loving freind

W Burley".

1 May 1573 Assembly

fol. 134r. 783 Robert Bonner, Alderman, took the oath as Mayor, Escheator, and Clerk of the Market before Richard Brigges the outgoing Mayor.

784 The Mayor received the following sums: £16 owed by Thomas Cleyborne of Lynn for a licence for 140 quarters of grain at 2s the quarter; also £24 and a bond for £24 by Richard Jefferay at Michaelmas next for another licence granted to Cleyborne for 400 quarters of grain at 2s the quarter; also £5 from Richard Brigges, late Mayor, owed by William Clark and Edward Gronte of Yarmouth and Theckenham [sic] in Norfolk for a similar licence.

Richard Brigges, Alderman, was elected a Justice of the Peace and a Justice of Common Pleas within the borough and took his oath. fol. 134v. 785

8 May 1573 Assembly

Agreed that Christopher Awdley, gentleman and Alderman, shall have for 21 years the government of "the Bekenage of the haven And Deepes of Boston" and shall lay sufficient "Bekenages boyes & Cannes" as are necessary to safeguard passengers and seafaring men. Awdley is to have all the profits of the passengers and wayfaring men and the corporation is to grant him £20 for his charges. He is to pay an annual rent of 12d and is bound in £100 to perform the terms of this agreement. 786 fol. 135r.

Robert Bonner, now Mayor, Thomas Doughtie, Alderman, and Richard Draper, one of the Common Council, have previously been leased by the corporation the profits of "the fyshyng above the Brigge" for a yearly rent. Because their fishing has been many times troubled by trees and other timber lying in the haven, it is agreed that they may have all the timber they can salvage, unless it is claimed by the owners within 24 days, who must pay reasonable charges to the farmers. 787

21 May 1573 Assembly

William Gannocke, Alderman, John Margery, Richard Draper, William Dallands and Thomas Derby, of the Common Council, failed to attend. fol. 135v. 788

At this assembly William Sisterson, one of the Common Council, promised within the next month to deliver to the corporation one hundred quarters of barley (at the rate of 120 quarters to the hundred) and 60 quarters of rye, at 13s 4d per quarter of barley and 16s every quarter of rye, to be "bestowed within the same Borughe by the wisdome & discressyon of the said maior and Burgesses". Sisterton is bound in £200 to the corporation to deliver the grain. 789 fol. 136r.

1 June 1573 Assembly

William Hawkrige and William Gannocke, Aldermen, failed to attend, though warned. 790

Agreed that Richard Faye shall have the supervision of all the grain brought to the borough by William Sisterson, storing the same in a convenient place, and selling it from time to time by the advice of the Mayor and Aldermen. He is to make account of all his proceedings and be recompensed by the corporation. 791

792 Thomas Hutchynson of Boston, barber, shall have the supervision and regulation of the "cuntry Ayle and bere" that is brought to the borough for sale at any victualling or tippling house, having the same profits as Thomas Wymbische of Boston, gent., lately had, for one year and paying 40s.

fol. 136v. [Copy of a letter to the corporation from Lord Burghley already transcribed on fol. 133v]

16 June 1574 [*sic*] *Assembly*

793 John Gawdrye, Alderman, John Margery, William Dallands, William Sisterson and Richard Draper failed to attend; the last four were fined 8d each.

fol. 137r.
794 Christopher Awdley, gent., has received from the corporation great sums of money towards the charges of "thaffaires & Business of this Burrowe", but has not yet made any account of them. He is now ordered to bring in this account in writing at the next Assembly provided that Mr Steven Thymolby, esquire, Recorder is present.

31 July 1574 [*sic*] *Assembly*

795 William Derby, esq., John Bell and William Gannocke, Aldermen, failed to attend, though summoned.

796 In consideration of £18 (to be paid by instalments), it is agreed to grant Martin Hunte a messuage and garden place in Boston lately
fol. 137v. occupied by Simon Paynter for 2d a year, together with suit of court at the great leets held at the Guildhall.

31 August 1573 Assembly

797 Agreed that a lease be made to Anthony Kyme, gent., Alderman, of the site of the "Austyn freres" with all the orchards and gardens, lately in the tenure of John Dove, deceased, of Boston; reserving to the corporation all trees growing there and also any surplus stone. The lease to be for 40 years, paying 100s for the first year and thereafter £6 13s 4d a year. The corporation is to have power of distraint and
fol. 138r. re-entry for non-payment of rent, and is to give notice of repairs which are to be done by the tenant. Kyme is to pay a fine of £10 at Midsummer 1574 and is not to assign the lease, except to his wife or children, without the consent of the corporation.

19 September 1573 Assembly

Philip Curtes, one of the Common Council, is appointed Bailiff and Collector of the town lands and revenues, including the Erection Lands, and also Bailiff of Husbandry for one year and so thereafter as the corporation and Curtes shall agree. Curtes shall be paid £10 a year and be given on entry to office a Rental listing all the corporation rents. Curtes is to make his account at the audit to be kept on Thursday in Whitsun week each year. fol. 138v. **798** fol. 139r.

22 September 1574 [*sic*] *Assembly*

Deed dated 2 May 1573 sealed for Peter Ferrer alias Pharo of one messuage together with a piece of land called Back Yard and a piece of land called a "Garth Stede" lying against the messuage in Butcher Row on the east side of the water. These lands were previously granted to Ferrer, but no assurance was made. With Ferrer's consent the corporation now by the present deed grants them by bargain and sale to Edward Blackwyn for ever for an annual rent of 4d, together with suit of court. **799** fol. 139v.

Deed dated 20 September 1573 sealed and delivered to the corporation by Thomas Doughtie, gent., Alderman, whereby he grants the Mayor and Burgesses in perpetuity all his tenement lately in decay and now reedified with the garden now enclosed on the west side of the water next to the late White Friars, and also the garden stede now enclosed by Thomas on the west side of his dwelling house, the inner part of the White Friars, and also a little lane leading from the highway to the White Friars. **800** fol. 140r.

Lease by the corporation for 300 years to Thomas Doughtie, in consideration of £15 paid, of all the properties specified in the previous entry with a yearly rent of 2d and suit of court to the manor of Halgarth. The corporation are to have "fre Egresse and Regresse with cart & carriages through the sayde lane unto the sayde Inner parte of the freeres to fetch or carrye away the stones within the said freeres which be now standinge in pillers or walles above the soyle or grownd of the same freers" except for the west wall of the inner part of the Friars. **801** fol. 140v. fol. 141r.

Mr Mayor, Simon Melsonbye, Mr Doughtie, George Erle, Andrew Leake, Richard Jefferay and Philip Curtes, or a majority of them, are appointed to assess the wages of the porters of the borough and what they take for carriage of wares and merchandise within the borough. **802**

803 In consideration of £18 to be paid by Martin Hunte of Boston, baker, the corporation has bargained and sold to him a messuage, garden and a half acre of pasture, lately held by Simon Paynter, to be held of the
fol. 141v. manor of Halgarth in socage, with a rent of 4d a year and suit of court. [see entry on fol. 137r.–v.]

804 Deed sealed for John Wilkynson for a stable in Butcher Row sold to him for £7, reserving suit of court and 1d rent per year.

10 October 1573 Assembly

805 William Watson, esquire, was elected Town Clerk according to an election made during the mayoralty of Master Brigges and took the oath. He "promised to be Resyaunte and Dwellinge in the Towne at or before Christmas nexte".

22 October 1573

806 Master Bell, Master Hawkrige, Aldermen, William Dallands, John Stamper, of the Common Council, neglected to attend. Others absent
fol. 142r. were pardoned or else had permission.

807 "At the same assemblie it is agreed that forasmuche as John Stamper haithe wilfullie disobeyed Mayster Maiors commaundmente and came not to his assemblie to answere suche thinges as there was to be Layde to his charge that he sholde paye for a fyne xx^{s} And at his home Cominge he shall upon summons geven hym appere before Mr Maior and the Justices of this Boroughe and there be bounde in a recognisance to reedifie and buylde againe the house that he pullyd downe in bargaite in as good forme as it is tennaundable accordinge to the Counselles Letter, and if he refuse so to doo then he to remaine in the Counter till he will be bounde to the same order".

808 "And it is agreed that the marte shalbe kepte in manner and forme hereaftrer followinge, in bargaite for horse bestes and shepe and other cattell and frome barbrige to the commen steathe for all merchaundise and fyshe and herringes to be kepte at the gaite".

809 John Slater is to have the Trinity Guildhall which he bought of the town; if he refuses to pay according to the bargain, he is to be sued.

26 October 1573 Assembly

810 Master Hawkrige, Alderman, and Andrew Leake, of the Common Council, were absent.

Agreed that John Stamper shall answer for the rebuilding of the house that he pulled down, by the return home of Master Thimolby the Recorder. 811

"At the same assemblie it is agreed that these foure hereafter to be named shalbe commissioners for the marte nexte insuinge to appoynte where every man shall stande with there cattell wares and fishe in manner and forme decently for a fayre and marte, that is to saye Thomas Orsbey and William Sisterson & they to have William Smithe and Richard Farnyl under theme". fol. 142v. 812

27 November 1573 Assembly

Deeds sealed: to Thomas Wryght for his house in the market place next to Leonard Bowshere's house with a cottage and a stable "as they were some tyme the priore and covente of Freston"; a lease for 21 years to John Stamper of a pasture containing three "stonges", for 5s per year, on condition Stamper fell no wood except the underwood for fencing, and the corporation have right of ingress to fell the timber. 813

Mr Gawdrye complained against Philip Curtes for "undecente wordes given to him abrode in the towne"; Curtes was fined 20s and "for his Imprisonemente it is refered to the comminge home of Mr Recorder". 814

18 December 1573 Assembly

Agreed to grant Ralph Pell, draper, a lease for 21 years of a house in the market place now in the tenure of Leonard Newsam, cordwainer, for 40s a year. Pell agrees to pay 40s to Thomas Symson, which Symson paid to Robert Barnes, baker, "for the good will of the said House with all suche charges as the said Symson can prove that he haythe layed forthe on it" fol. 143r. 815

29 December 1573 Assembly

William Gannocke, Alderman, John Margery and Ralph Pell, of the Common Council, failed to attend. 816

Agreed that no person in the borough serve or tipple country ale, except John Cartwright, Ralph Pell, William Aldaies, Edward Austyll, Roger Browne, William Dixon, Robert Barnes, Ralph Spurre and Widow Kelsay. Also none to serve country beer or ale except Andrew Leake, Peter Pantrie, John Stamper, Margaret Browne, William Dallands, John Woode, Francis Hoode. Those offending against this order are to pay 3s for every dozen of ale or kilderkin of beer drawn. Also "that the imprest money paide for aile & bere shall from this daye sease and the brewers to have halfe of all forfittes". 817

3v. 18 A letter was read from Mr Sapcottes for the arrears of £6 13s 4d and 10s for a sequestration and 5s 8d for the Exchequer. Agreed to send it by "the firste that comithe".

[*12 January 1573/4 Assembly*]

819 "Also at this assemblie holden the xijth of January was nomynated to have the oversighte of the pore Mr Clement and George Erle Richard Draper and John Wilkinson"

16 January 1573/4 Assembly

820 "At this assemblie caime Cristopher Awdley one of the Aldermen of the said Borroughe and in oppen courte before the said Maior Aldermen and Common Counsell of the said Borroughe, being examined by the said Maior, did oppenlie confesse with a penitente harte and lowlie submission that he had committed advowtrie and fornicacion within the said Borroughe, upon whose confession, the said Maior Aldermen and Common Counsell haithe with one consente consydering the same offence to be most odious before god and also so shamefull in this worlde to the discredet of this howse and the worshipfull companye of the same have at this instante dismissed the said Cristopher of the companye of an Alderman and likwise of the liberties of this howse.

821 And furdermore the said Maior by vertue of the Quenes Majesties graunte and Letters pattentes graunted to the said Maior and Burgesses of the said Borrough for the correccion and punishmente of suche offence in the presence of the Aldermen and Common Counsell above named consydring the said Christopher was an Alderman within the said Borroughe and what slaunders mighte ensew to the said Maior Aldermen and worshipfull companye of the encorporation of the said Borroughe if he sholde putte the said Cristofer to open punishmente for the same offence and also for that he found the said Cristofer to have grete repentaunce and that he did willinglie submitt hym selfe and assente to suche punishment as the said Maior wolde
fol. 144r. appoynte And allso for divers other grete causes of repentaunce which did appeare in the said Cristopher Therefore the Said Maior aswell the promisses considered as for divers other good causes & reasonable considerations thym specially moving did refuse to putt the said Cristopher to open punishmente but was content to punnish him by *pena pecuniaria* And hathe appoynted and assessed the said Cristofer to paye for his said offence the some of v^{li} of lawfull Englishe moneye to be imployed to the use of the pore within the same Borroughe at the discrecion of the Maior and aldermen of the same boroughe or the most parte of theme which some of v^{li} the said Cristofer haithe presentlye paide to the hands of the said Maior to thuse above named".

26 February 1573/4 Assembly

William Derby esquire, one of the Alderman has "fallen into grete Decaye by reason whereof he haithe bene longe absent" from this House, and is therefore dismissed from aldermanic office. **822**

Thomas Derby of the Common Council was likewise dismissed for the same cause. **823**

Richard Feilde of the Common Council was chosen Alderman in place of Christopher Awdley, previously dismissed. **824**

George Erle of the Common Council was chosen Alderman in place of William Derby. **825**

5 March 1573/4 Assembly: Ember Day

John Bell, Alderman, and Thomas Owrsbye of the Common Council were absent, but came later and were pardoned. fol. 144v. **826**

Richard Feilde and George Erle took the oath as Aldermen. **827**

12 March 1573/4 Assembly

Christopher Cowper and Thomas Robynson were sworn as members of the Common Council. **828**

John Hiltoft, gent., was admitted and sworn a freeman and was also sworn as one of the Common Council. **829**

It was agreed that from next Lady Day two of the Common Council shall be chosen each year to be the "collectors and Receyvers of the hole Revenuer issues & profittes aswell of the ereccion Landes as of all other the landes what soever belonging to this Borroughe". One bailiff is to be responsible for the Erection lands and those given by Mistress Fox and her late husband Master Fox, at a yearly salary of 33s 4d. The other is to be responsible for the remaining lands at a yearly salary of 53s 4d. Both bailiffs while they hold office and afterwards shall be exempt from service as constable, dikegraves and alefounder. Anyone elected as bailiff who refuses to serve will be fined 40s. **830**

Andrew Leake was chosen Bailiff of the Erection lands and Richard Jefferay for the other lands during the coming year. fol. 145r. **831**

25 March 1574 Assembly

Simon Melsonbye, Anthony Kyme and Richard Feilde, Aldermen, were put in election for the mayoralty and Anthony Kyme, having the most voices, was chosen. "God sende hym ioye". **832**

30 March 1574 Assembly

833 Simon Turpyn has bought of the corporation a piece of void ground at Wormgate for 30s.

834 The corporation has sold to Richard Feilde an annual rent of 15s on his dwelling house in the west, for a payment of £13. He is to hold the same house at 1d rent in free socage and suit of court to the manor of Hussy Hall.

9 April 1574 Assembly

835 The following deeds were sealed: a bond under the common seal to pay £100 to Martin Erle, gent., on 8 April 1575; a lease for 21 years of 2 acres in Boston at a yearly rent of 6s to John Fox; a lease for 300 years to Thomas Doughtie of a tenement on the west side of the water against William Wesname's messuage for 1d rent; a lease for 21 years to Ralph Pell of a messuage on the east side of the water near the market place, for 40s per annum.

836 Simon Turpyn was sold a piece of void ground at Wormgate for 30s paid down.

837 There was "tolde and tendred" £200 in money and gold and all the plate and jewels given by the will of Thomas Browne, esquire, deceased, to Dorothy his daughter in the presence of Richard Brigges and John Browne, executors of the will. They "refused the receyte thereof and there was none there to receyve the same".

23 April 1574 Assembly

838 A recognisance has been forfeitted by Edward Forster and his sureties Robert Bryan and Thomas Dolby due to Edward's non-appearance at Michaelmas sessions. But because he has not broken the Queen's peace since making the recognisance and has submitted himself to the Mayor and Justices of the borough, only 40s shall be forfeited.

839 Richard Draper is chosen and sworn Coroner and shall continue until discharged by this House.

840 The fine of 20s on Philip Curtes for an abuse against Mr Gawdrye and the referral of his punishment to the next coming of the Recorder is remitted.

26 April 1574 Assembly
It was agreed to grant to William Closse, tanner, a lease for 21 years of his dwelling house and buildings there, with an acre of pasture and piece of land late Lord Roos', abutting on the haven to the east, at an annual rent of 33s 4d and for a fine of 20s. **841**

28 April 1574 Assembly
"At this assemblie yt was agreed by the Maior and Comon Counsell that whereas Cristopher Audley gent ys to marrye and to take to wife one Mrs. Busshey who cannot as yet be wonne to inhabite within this Borough unles the said Cristopher Audley can obtayne oure graunte under our common seale to be discharged of the maioraltye and of all other offyce beringe within the said Boroughe duringe her naturall life althoughe the said Corporacion be verie unwillinge to have any suche graunte or presidente to be showed against theme althoughe they mighte gayne mutche more thereby yet consideringe yt standeth upon the prefermente of the said Cristopher to have the said graunte for the satisfying of the desyer of the said gentlewoman and for that the said corporacion is gretley bounden to gratify the said Christopher Awdly by whome it haithe received so many and grete benefittes and tokens of favour and good will as by noo inhabitante more, and for that we hope in tyme the said gentylwoman maybe otherwyes perswaded. Therfore the premisses consydered being loothe to for goo the companye of the said Cristopher for the cause above said yt is now therfore at this assemblie fullie accorded graunted and agreed that the said Cristopher shall at no tyme duringe the said intermariage with the said Mrs Busshey be compelled and inforced to beare any office within the said borough butt to be clearly discharged thereof as well of the maioralty as of all other office bearinge, within the said Borowe whatsoever without the free assente and consente of the said Mris Busshey firste obteyned to be showed in wryttinge to the Maior there for the tyme beinge". fol. 146v. **842**

[copy of the preceding order] fol. 147r.

License by the Mayor and Burgesses of Boston exempting Christopher Awdley, gent., from having to bear the office of Mayor or any other office within the borough during the time of his dwelling there and during his marriage to Elizabeth Busshey, gentlewoman, unless Elizabeth gives her written consent. **843** fol. 147v.

blank fol. 148r.

fol. 149v. *blank*

4 June 1574 Assembly

844 "It is agreed at this assemble that the Churche of Saint Johannis in the sowthend of Boston shalbe repayred & amended with all Convenient Spede & that ther shalbe wekelye Sarvice ther done by a mynyster Commonlye called the Maiors Chapleyne That is to say the Sondaye the Wensdaye & the Frydaye every weeke And that there shalbe a Common Sessement maide amongst the Inhabitaunces of this Borrowhe for the charge of the same with all Convenient Spede".

845 John Bell and William Gannocke neglected to attend.

846 John Garrat, smith, shall have the purchase of a tenement and garden in Bargate rented at 20s a year. He is to pay £13 6s 8d, together with 2d a year and suit of court to the manor of Hallgarth.

847 Agreed there should be a fold made on the west side of the water for keeping of distresses.

3 July 1574 Assembly

fol. 149v John Margery and William Dallands of the Common Council failed to
848 attend.

849 Deeds sealed: for a houe sold to John Garrocke; and a letter of attorney to Andrew Leake and Richard Jeferay to collect all sums due to them.

20 July 1574 Assembly

850 John Matson having been called on for a debt of £6 due by his predecessor, on John's suit to the Assembly it was agreed that he should pay 20s in hand, 20s next Christmas, 40s at Christmas 1575 and 40s at Christmas 1576. He is to be bound in £4 for each sum of 40s.

851 It was agreed to procure a commission of the sewers for the borough next Michaelmas Term.

852 Agreed to sue for the Lord Admiral's release of Admiralty rights at the next Term.

Lord Clinton is to have a patent of the Stewardship of the borough to enjoy it in reversion after his father's death, with a fee of £10. 853

"At this assemble yt is agreed that Mr Bell may be tollerated to be absent for one hole yere next after the date herof & that uppon this condicion that he shall beare all the charges as an alderman within this Borrowghe & after the yeares ende the licence to Seace & that yt is lawfull for the Maior & Burgesses to proceade to the election of a new Justice in his rowme provided allway that he shall be attendant of Master Maior at the hall uppon speciall Cause and warnynge gyven to hym". 854

1 September 1574 Assembly

Mr Doughtie, Alderman, and Mr Hiltoft and Ralph Pell, of the Common Council, were absent. 855

The nomination of William Kyme, gent., as Town Clerk was agreed fol. 150r.
by the following persons: Simon Turpyn, Robert Turpyn, Andrew Leake, Philip Curtes, Thomas Owrsbye, John Stamper, William Dallands, John Fox, of the Common Council, and George Erle, Richard Feilde, Robert Bonner, Thomas Thorye, Anthony Claymonde, Richard Brigges, John Gawdrye, Simon Melsonbye, Aldermen, and Anthony Kyme, gent., Mayor. On condition that he remains and dwells in the borough. 856

13 September 1574 Assembly

It is agreed that the great horse bought to serve the town should be sold to the highest bidder. The purchaser shall be bound to provide the town with an able horse when needed or pay as much as the horse is estimated to be worth. 857

William Kyme, the Town Clerk, took his oath. 858

17 September 1574 Assembly: in the absence of the Mayor

Mr Anthony Kyme, Mayor, Thomas Thorye, Alderman, Richard Draper, John Stamper, Richard Jefferay, Andrew Leake, Edmund Tonyton, John Hiltoft, Robert Turpyn, Ralph Pell, and William Sisterson were absent. 859

17 September 1574 Assembly: in the presence of the Mayor

Agreed that Mr Anthony Kyme, Mayor, should have the horse bought for the town together with its equipment for the sum of £7. 860

17 December 1574 Assembly

fol. 150v.

861 "At this assembly it is agreed & ordered by Mr Maior thaldermen and Comon Councell of this Borrowe of Boston upon informacion made by Mr Melsonbye one of the Justices of Peace within the sayd Borrowe and John Harcastell one of the fremen of this Borrowe made unto the sayd Maior and Aldermen of dyvers evell & opprobrius wordes and mysdemenors spoken Commytted & Done by Thomas Wright one of the fremen there agaynst thaldermen & the state thereof unreverentlye and contrarye to his Dewtye &c that the said Thomas Wryght shall be Commytted to warde without bayle and maynprise & that his mysdemenors shall be put in wryting and Certefyed unto the Councell & for further orders to be with him taken for his sayd misordered mysdemenors by ther wysdomes".

862 Agreed that William Sisterson shall have the reversion of the lease of a messuage of 17 acres in Donington in the tenure of John Wryght after a survey has been made.

20 December 1574 Assembly

863 A letter of attorney was sealed and delivered to Mr Alexander Skynner, gent., to receive all bonds due to the Mayor and Burgesses for the shipment of 2000 quarters of grain from the ports of Lynn and Yarmouth or their members.

864 Three licences sealed at this Assembly for the transporting of grain: one to George Farfax, Richard Farfax, Henry Skynner and Andrew Leake dated 18 December 1574 for the shipment of 1000 quarters from Boston and its members; another to John Broke, John Hutton, James Atkyn of London, merchant, and [*blank*] of Lynn dated the same day for the shipment of 1000 quarters from Lynn and Yarmouth; and another to John Broke, John Hutton, Thomas Grave, Thomas Cleyborne, Francis Shakton and John Waydson dated the same day

fol. 151r.

for the shipment of 1000 quarters from Lynn and Yarmouth. In the presence and with the consent of Mr Anthony Kyme, Mayor, Simon Melsonbye, John Gawdrye, Richard Brigges, Anthony Claymonde, and George Erle, Aldermen, Richard Jefferay, John Fox, John Hiltoft, and Andrew Leake, Burgesses.

27 December 1574 Assembly

865 A letter of attorney was sealed to receive bonds for debts due to the corporation for 1200 quarters of licence money, constituting William Ashwell, gent., and John Raynes, gent., of Lynn attorneys. In the presence of Anthony Kyme, Mayor, Simon Melsonbye, Richard Brigges, and William Hawkrige, Aldermen.

22 January 1574/5 Assembly
Deputations for buying corn dated 18 December 1574 were sealed: to John Harvarde, John Haynes and Thomas Beste for 160 [?quarters]; to John Chatters for 100; to Thomas Fare for 100; to Richard Berrye and Edward Ryddesdale for 260; to Henry Cobot for 100; to John Broke, John Hutton, Gamalliel Wexford and Nicholas Darby for 200. Sum total: 1900 [?quarters]. There remains 100 [?quarters] for Andrew Leake and Mr Darbye. **866**

25 February 1574/5 Assembly fol. 151v.
John Gawdrye and Andrew Leake failed to attend. **867**

Anthony Claymonde, William Gannocke, and Thomas Owrsbye were excused attendance. **868**

It is ordered that the orders concerning attendance on the Mayor by the Aldermen and Common Council at certain days should be entered into the book of orders and likewise the orders for wearing of livery gowns. **869**

23 March 1574/5 Assembly
John Bell, Thomas Doughtie and Richard [*blank*], Aldermen, and John Margery, William Dallands, John Hiltoft, Robert Turpyn and Simon Turpyn, of the Common Council, failed to attend. **870**

25 March 1575 Assembly
Simon Melsonbye, John Bell, William Hawkrige, Anthony Claymonde, Thomas Thorye, Wiliam Gannocke, Richard Feilde and George Erle were in election for the mayoralty. Out of these Gannocke, Feilde and Erle were chosen for a further election and Feilde was chosen. **871**

Alderman Richard Feilde was absent. **872**

John Harcastell was elected to the Common Council in place of Edmund Toynton, "departed", and took his oath. **873**

16 April 1575 Assembly
Lord Clinton's patent for the office of High Steward of the manors, lands etc. of the borough of Boston was sealed, with a fee of £10 yearly, and also a grant of "all fishes Ryall and wreck of the sea" within the haven and liberties. fol. 152r. **874**

The "Rede booke" containing the copy of the charters of the corporation was delivered to Christopher Awdley to take to London for the defence of the privileges of the borough. He promises to bring it back "safe and unhurt or Defaced" when he returns. **875**

876 John Hiltoft, gent., was elected an Alderman in the place of William Hawkrige, deceased, and took the oath.

fol. 152v. *blank*

1 May 1575 Assembly

877 Mr Richard Feilde took the oath as Mayor.

2 May 1575 Assembly

878 It was agreed to seal a certificate concerning the punishment of Christopher Awdley, late Alderman, for incontinency.

879 It was recorded that one bill obligatory dated 1 September 1572 remained in the Guildhall by which William Derby, esquire, is bound in £20 to Richard Brigges, Alderman.

880 A copy of a letter sent by Anthony Kyme, late Mayor, and Alexander Skynner, Customer of the port, to the Privy Council:
"ower Dewtyes unto your honors moste humbly Remembred, where as certen Robbers frequenting the coastes of Lincoln Shyer do now lye att this presente in the Depes or mouthe of Boston havon not onely
fol. 153v. to the greate discurraging of honest Marchauntes But allso to thutter overthrowe of all trade in these partyes, and further where as we have apprehended iiij of the said cumpanye & by there Examynacions fynding them to be pyrates have comytted theme to warde according to theffect of the Quenes Majesties proclaimacion Anno xi^mo^ in that behalf provyded we according to our bounden Dewtyes have thought good to certefye thus much to your Honours whereby we may Receyve your Lordship's further direccons therin we be in dowbte what order to take with the said prisoners, and thus we beseche allmightye god to preserve your good Lordship in helth & honor frome Boston this last of Aprill

your honors must humble att
Commaundement
Anthony Kyme Maior
Alexander Skynner Thomas Bennytt
Collectors Robert Townley Comptroller
Simon Melsonby John Gawdry and
Richard Brigges Aldermen and Justices

To the Right Honorable & our Singler good Lordes the Lordes of the Quenes most honorable Counsell".

Memorandum: 45s 4d and 10s of freedom money (6s 8d from Hendy and 3s 4d from Wood) was taken out of the Court box and delivered to Anthony Kyme, late Mayor. 881

Agreed that the serjeants have 40s per annum for fees and wages, paid quarterly. 882

"Item att thys assembly yt ys fully agreed by the hole house that this corporacon shall stond in contencon with the Towne of Lynne for the fredome of the towle of this Borrowe & that there shalbe processe procured agenst one Henry Hill the tolle getherer of Lynn for certen Distresses by hym taken of this townes men owte of the courte of Duchye chawmbers off Lancaster & the matter to be followed with effect". 883

A note of Lord Clinton's letter to the Mayor and Burgesses of Boston fol. 154r.
for the delivery of certain pirates 3 May 1576: 884
"Mr Maior Whereas I have understonding that yow have charged your Selves with the custodye of certen prisoners which are suspected of pyracye, whose causes ar not triable nor Determynable within your Severall Jurisdiccions but before the highe Admirall of Englond & his Deputyes, lawfully authorysed, I have therefore commaunded myne officers & Marshall to take theme into his custodye and Receyve them at your hands, Excepte yow have Aucthorytye for the Justefyeng of there keping in prison that yow maye Warrant the same bye, and so Referring yt to yower Discressyon, I leve to truble yow herein enny further
frome Tatteshall this ij^{d} of Maye
your verye loving
frende H Clynton
To my very loving frendes Mr Maior & the Justices of the burrowe of Boston deliver theise".

Memorandum: 4 May 1575. Richard Pharo, Robert Gildon and James West, tallowchandlers, came before the Mayor and Justices in the Guildhall to ask them to set a price for the sale of their candles during the coming year. They were limited to the following prices: candles with cotton wicks 3½d per pound and candles with other wicks 3d per pound. 885

13 May 1575 Assembly

886 John Bell, Alderman, and John Margery of the Common Council failed to attend, though warned.

887 Mr Richard Feilde, Mayor, Simon Melsonbye, John Gawdrye, Richard Brigges, Anthony Claymonde, Robert Bonner, Aldermen,
fol. 154v. and Thomas Owresby, Andrew Leake, William Dallands and Richard Draper, are appointed to survey St John's church concerning repairs, and to make assessments on the inhabitants for the cost of the repairs.

888 "At thys Assembly yt ys agreed & ordered by Mr Maior thaldermen & comen counsell of this burrowe that the Ayle & Beare Brewers of the same Burrowe, before there beare & Ayle be Tonned shall send for the ayle conners of this burrowe to take taste of ther beare and Ayle & to se that the same be good & wholsome drinck & that they shall sell there beare & Ayle at resonable prises Afte the Rate as malte ys & shalbe solde in the market & that they shall brewe & putt to sale in this towne no bere but merchaunte beare and single Beare & that they shall not sell there merchaunt Beare above ij[d] the gallon nor there single beare Above xx[d] the kylderkyn".

889 Agreed that no victualler or tippler of the borough shall henceforth sell any beer or ale brewed outside this town, but only beer and ale brewed within the borough, on pain of 2s 6d per kilderkin and 12d for every pot of ale. The Mayor is to appoint a Collector to collect the fines. This order take effect from next Whitsuntide.

27 May 1575 Assembly

890 William Gannocke, Alderman, failed to attend, though warned.

891 With the consent of the beer brewers, the following prices are agreed:
fol. 155r. double beer at 4s the kilderkin; merchant beer "verye good" 2s 8d the kilderkin; and single beer for 20d the kilderkin. The brewers undertake to serve the whole town at these prices.

892 By like order the ale brewers are to sell their best ale at 3d the gallon and not to refuse to serve any townsman at that price. This order is to take effect 12 days after this Assembly and thereafter no innkeeper or victualler may sell any beer other than that brewed in the borough at the agreed prices.

Memorandum: a letter dated 14 June was sent to Mr Thomas Cecil[27] by William Dyneley concerning a deputation of certain corn licensed to be transported by the corporation: **893**
"Ower humble commendacions to your worshuppe Remembred singnefyeng unto the same that we have Receyved your letters by Mr Anthonye Kyme towching the Lycens off vj^{m} quarters of grane which was graunted to your worshypp in the tyme of his mayoraltye, whereapon we have considered & thereapon be fully agreed, meaning by godes grace to accomplyshe the same in such convenyent tyme as we maye, In the meane tyme we are to crave of your mastership such reasonable consideracion for our monnye, So as yf yt myght be possible we have the hole Some for the furnature of our greate charges in hand, and yf not then thone half in hand, and thother half at mychelmes or martynmes next, at the furthest meaning never the lesse to geve you such tyme for your transportacion as by our lycence we maye, Thus craving your Worshypps Resolucion by this bearer with suche convenyent Spede as you maye that thereapon we may forthwith send to your Worshypp ower Deputacion. We commytt yow unto the proteccion of thallmightye frome Boston this xiiij of June
Your Worshypps to use Richard Feilde Maior".

14 June 1575 Assembly

William Gannocke, Alderman, and Andrew Leake and John Margery, of the Common Council, failed to attend though warned. fol. 155v **894**

It was agreed to seal and send to Mr Thomas Cecil as promised the deputation for transporting grain. **895**

Note of a letter sent to Mr Kyme by Mr Thomas Cecil 1575: **896**
"Mr Kyme I dyd looke to have of my licence frome the Towne of Boston, sithens yowr going Downe. I pray yow let yt be sent up by some trustye messinger And as towching the payment of the monnye, I will stond bounden to paye the thre hundrethe poundes which ys dewe for Syx thousand quarters by a hundreth poundes Everye yere, and to pay in thre yeres everye halfe yere fyftye pounds, for as this yere falleth owte, I meane not to make yt awaye And yet I wyl begynne to make my fyrst payment att Christmas next Dated the viijth of June
Your assured frend
Tho. Cecill".

[27] Thomas Cecil (1542–1622), eldest son of William Cecil; 2nd Lord Burghley, later Earl of Exeter.

897 Note of the answer sent to Mr Cecil:
"Ryght Worshupfull our Dewtye to your Worshippe Remembred, We have Recyved your letters of the viijth of June last whereby we do perceyve that yow ar desyrus to have the lycence of vj^{m} Quarters of grane sent unto yow, and that for the same yow ar contented to make of ccc^{li} in thre yere, our bargane with Mr Kyme was xij^{d} for Everye quarter which after the Rate of vj score quarters to everye hundrethe Amounteth to the some of ccclx^{li}, and to have a moytye or at the leaste a Thyrd parte in hand, which we be willing for yow to accomplishe, And nowe perceyving by your letter that yow wolde pay the same but in thre yeres, we ar moste humbly to Request you to consider of ower
fol. 156r. woorkes begoone, & our presente necessytye for the same. Whych we be not able to fynyshe withoute Some ayde Wherefore yf yt myght please yow to helpe us with so miche monnye as you convenyently may in hand we wilbe contented to be the longer for our latter paymentes, And for your lycence we will send yt unto yow by one that we meane to send to yow for that purpos, & for Recept of your monny, so knowethe thalmyghtye who preserve yow in much worshup, from boston the xviijth of June yor worshupp

Richard Feylde maior sub
Sigillo officii".

3 July 1575 Assembly

898 William Gannocke and Thomas Doughtie, Aldermen, and Andrew Leake of the Common Council failed to attend, though warned.

899 It is ordered that Richard Jesse, William Dyxon and Richard Turner shall be pinders for the west side of the water for the coming year and have for "a Stray grene" an acre of ground at Furthend which they shall fence, so that the cattle put there do not annoy the neighbours' grounds, for a yearly rent of 10s 8d.

900 Richard Jesse was made a freeman and took the oath.

14 July 1575 Assembly

901 Richard Jesse was elected to the Common Council and the serjeants were commanded to give him summons to attend the next Assembly to take his oath.

16 July 1575 Assembly

902 John Bell, John Gawdrye, William Gannocke and John Hiltoft, Aldermen, failed to attend, though warned.

fol. 156v.
903 Richard Jesse took his oath as a member of the Common Council.

Thomas Owresby, Richard Jefferay, Andrew Leake, William Dallands, Thomas Robynson, and John Wilkynson were appointed sessors for the repair of the church. 904

23 July 1575 Assembly

John Bell and William Gannocke, Aldermen, failed to attend, though warned. 905

It was ordered that George Farfax, weekly tenant of two cellars with the chambers over them, should no longer be farmer of them and should relinquish possession within 14 days, upon warning. 906

The deputation to Thomas Derby and Harry Skynner for transporting 1000 quarters of grain dated 29 June 1575 was sealed. 907

Anthony Kyme, gent., and Alexander Skynner, gent., are to have a deputation sealed for the transporting of 2000 quarters of grain from Lynn previously granted to Mr Thomas Cecil, to be transported by persons nominated by Anthony and Alexander. 908

At the request of the said Anthony and Alexander another deputation is to be sealed for 3000 quarters of grain on the behalf of Mr Cecil. The grain is to be shipped from Boston, Lynn and Yarmouth, 1000 quarters from Lincolnshire, the rest from Norfolk. This makes up the 6,000 quarters granted to Mr Thomas Cecil at 12d the quarter. Consequently, Anthony and Alexander have sealed and delivered to the corporation six bonds dated 21 July 1575 for the payment of £360, by half-yearly instalments of £60. On condition that the toll on the grain be paid. 909 fol. 157r.

"An Assembly had etc. the xxiiith day of July in the yere afforesaid"

Four deputations sealed for transporting 500 quarters of grain each, and another one for transporting 2000 quarters, all to be shipped from ports in Norfolk. Another deputation also of 1000 quarters for shipment from Boston, which with the deputation for 1000 quarters above written, amounts to the sum of 6000 quarters of grain granted to Sir Thomas Cecil. 910

Memorandum: one deputation of 500 quarters for Lynn is cancelled and in recompense two other deputations were sealed dated 22 July 1575 (one to Thomas Cleyborne for 100 quarters, another to unknown persons for 400 quarters).

911 Copy of a letter sent to the Mayor from Sir Thomas Cecil:
"Mr Maior I commend Right herteley to yow And to yor Bretherne, And where as a graunte ys maid betwyxt us for thre yeres Daye of ccclx[li] to be payd at Syx payments halfyerely, the fyrst payment whereof to begynne at michelmes next by obligacons to be sealed unto yow by Anthonye Kyme & Alyx[r] Skynner, these ar to Desyer yow that yow wyll Depute such under yowr Seale off Corporacion as they will have, according to my Lords direccion, unto Lynne porte for ye
fol. 157v. quantytye of towe thousand quarters, licence And to Thomas Derby & henry Skynner for one thousand in Boston porte, Requyring aswell for divers consderacions very necessarye to be weyd, As allso for the Shortning of the payments which I willingly wyshe were paid in one yere (yf no just occacyon hynder the same) that yow will not onely favour the passage as much as with your wisdoms semeth Expedyent, wherby I may the sooner be owte of debte, and yow in short tyme payd, but allso have regarde that sinester Reportes & sedicyus Styrrers of Sedicions in that cause, be not causelesse incurraged comforted nor borne withall, to your owne displeasers & hynderances as of late (yf yow had not wysely Repressed the same) yt woulde have come to passe, And thus confirming what so ever the said Anthony and Alexander shall do in my behalf therein, with Request as leysur may serve yow to consider of your owne warff nedefull to be Repayred Adionying to two of your poore neybors muche hyndered thereby, as the alledge called Systerson & Andrewe the brewer I betake yow to the tuicion of thalmightye frome Tattersall this xxij[th] of July 1575
I pray yow Remember to make over thother thre thousand quarters parcell of the Syx thousand by Letter of deputacon to Mr Kyme & Mr Skyner or to such whome they shall appoynte, for the which yow ar to take there bond for the thre hundred & threscore poundes

Your loving frend
Thomas Cicell"

29 July 1575 Assembly

912 It was agreed that John Bell, Alderman, and one of the Justices of the Peace, is with his own consent discharged from the office of Justice. Anthony Claymonde, Alderman, was chosen in his place and took the oath.

fol. 158r. Memorandum: 30 July 1575 Alexander Skynner, gent., paid to Mr
913 Richard Feilde, Mayor, £18, part of 2000 quarters of grain of John Broke's reckoning for transporting it out of Norfolk.

30 July 1575 Assembly
John Gawdrye, Anthony Claymonde, William Gannocke and Anthony Kyme, Aldermen, failed to attend, though warned. **914**

William Dallands, Richard Draper, Andrew Leake, Christopher Cowper, Thomas Robynson and William Smyth, of the Common Council, also failed to attend. **915**

A note of a letter from the Privy Council to the Mayor and Burgesses concerning certain pirates apprehended at Boston. Commendations for their diligence in apprehending the pirates. They are to give notice of their proceedings to Lord Clinton, the Vice-Admiral in those parts, and to send to him all the examinations they have taken, so that Clinton can determine the matter. Dated 8 March 1575 and signed Burghley, Lincoln, Sussex, Leicester, Knolles, Crofte, and Smythe. **916**

7 August 1575 Assembly
Agreed that John Bell, late Alderman and Justice, should be fully discharged from those offices, but his freedom is respited. fol. 158v. **917**

26 August 1575 Assembly
Anthony Claymonde and Thomas Doughtie, Aldermen, and John Stamper, Andrew Leake, and Thomas Robynson of the Common Council failed to attend, though warned. The Aldermen were pardoned. **918**

It was agreed to set a lock on the door to the cellars in the tenure of George Farfax, merchant, to prevent him entering them, until such time as he reaches agreement with the corporation and pays the rent due for them. **919**

23 September 1575 Assembly
Ralph Pell, of the Common Council, failed to attend, though warned; the others that made default were pardoned. **920**

It was agreed that all money now owed for the communion wine should be paid by the churchwardens out of their collection. In future the wine will be paid for yearly by the farmer of the parsonage of Boston, who will receive 6d per week from the inhabitants according to custom. **921**

Alan Manby and Thomas Winsper, Wardens of the Corporation of Tailors, delivered to Mr Mayor 6s 8d for the profits of their corporation. fol. 159r. **922**

923 Thomas Winsper and William Colman (previously chosen Wardens of their company) and William Hutchenson, elected Beadle, took their oaths of office.

26 October 1575 Assembly

924 Agreed that John Browne should be Solicitor for the borough in the actions brought by the corporation in the courts of Exchequer and Duchy Chamber concerning the toll claimed against them by the town of Lynn. In this matter Mr Shyttelworth, the town's counsellor, and Mr Guyenes, their attorney, are to be made privy, because they have "yntreated" against Harry Hyll of Lynn.

925 Agreed that one of the Serjeants at Mace shall ride to London to receive £37 from Mr Cecil and £24 of John Launde, butcher, and with it pay Mr Awdley £44 and bring the residue home.

14 November 1575 Assembly

fol. 159v. John Fox, Thomas Owresby, and Andrew Leake were put in election
926 for aldermanic office, and Thomas Owresby was elected. William Smyth was elected to the Common Council.

26 November 1575 Assembly

927 Agreed that every inhabitant, in the high street and all the back lanes, shall every night during the market hang a lighted lantern in his house to give light to passers by, from 6 pm until 9 pm. Offenders to be fined 12d for each default; the Beadles to report on offenders. The order to take effect from St Andrew's eve.

928 Agreed that about ten persons with harness and halberts shall attend on the Mayor continually during the duration of the market each year in order to keep the Queen's peace.

fol. 160r. "Articles obiected ayenst Lennerd Cracrofte esquyer the Daye & yere
929 afforsaid

fyrst the said Lennerd said that yf ennye alderman were in his howse he wolde tye his hede to a Block

Item yt ys Reported he sholde Saye that yf he had an alderman owte of this Towne he hoped to have hym by the heeles, althoughe he were as greate as a Justice of peace.

Item he hath Reported that the corporacion ys forfeted, and that the maior Justices & aldermen were knaves & Delt Knavyshlye.

Item the said Cracrofte With his menne att his heeles made an assaute of Robert Bonner one of thaldermen of This towne & his wyfe & went aboute with his Stone bowe to kyll his pyggyence contrarye to the laws.

Item he was comaunded (for avoyding of greate Inconvenyences) that nether he nor his men sholde wore Ennye weapons Disorderlye, and yet neverthelesse in contempte of the said comaundment both he & his men dyd were there weapons within this burrowe att extraordynarye howers & verye disorderly contrarye to the Quenes Peace".

"Item yt ys att this Assembly agreed by the maiore aldermen & comon Counsell of this burrowe that the marte begynning att St Andrewes Daye Which shalbe in the yere of our Lorde 1576 shalbe Kepte of the west syde of the Water of this Burrowe & so for ij yeres after that viz. for thre yerez in the whole, And that All Marchauntes & artifycers bringing wares to be solde within the said marte shall take Shoppes wheare to put there wares to sale And shalle not sett upp ennye bothes for that purpos so Long as they may have ennye Shoppes or warehouse for ennye Reasonable monnye During the said marte". **930**

Memorandum: on a question to Mr Steven Thymolby, Recorder, whether the Mayor and Justices at sessions of the peace may on the presentment of offences assess the fines of the offenders and make out process *pro fine*. His opinion is that on every presentment where the party presented is not admitted to his traverse, they may do so. fol. 160v. **931**

2 December 1575 Assembly

Agreed that henceforth persons coming to the town at market time or during the time of the fairs shall be free from legal actions proceeding from the borough court of pleas, although not exempt from actions in the court of piepowder concerning any business or contract made at the market or fair, unless the Mayor and two Justices decide to the contrary. **932**

9 December 1575 Assembly

It was agreed to grant Thomas Cleyborne for £20 a new licence for 400 quarters of grain, he bringing in his old deputation for 200 quarters of grain which he has transported. **933**

934 Memorandum: 15 September 1575 another deputation was sealed for Thomas Cleyborne to transport 400 quarters of grain (except wheat),
fol. 161r. that is for 240 quarters, part of 400 quarters granted by a previous licence, which is now brought in and cancelled. Now he has licence for 200 quarters more, for which he has paid £20 at the sealing of the licence and 40s more for renewing his former deputation. £22 was this day delivered to Edward Jeffrey for the corporation.

20 December 1575 Assembly

935 Copy of a letter from Lord Clinton to the Mayor in favour of Thomas Burbanck:

"Mr Maior I think yow understand that this manne hath bene hardly Delt withall more for mallyce & the plesure of hym which was last your maior, than for Enny Just cause wherefore these ar to desyer yow to showe him as muche favor as yow canne, wherein yow shall do a very good Dede & funde me thankfulle, so with my hartye comendacions I byd yow farewell, from horncastell this xiij^th^ off Decembr 1575

Your assured freind
E Clynton".

936 It was agreed to provide six hooks for pulling down houses in case of staithe fires.

937 It was also ordered that every Alderman should have in his keeping a ladder with 12 staves, and also every member of the Common Council for the necessary occasions of the borough.

938 Simon Melsonbye and John Gawdrye, Aldermen, Richard Draper, Richard Jefferay, Simon Turpyn, William Sisterson and Matthew Freyston are to survey the banks in the Holmes and appoint every man's part in the repairing of the sea dike.

939 Answer to Lord Clinton's letter:

"Ryght honerable our dewtyes Remembered yt may please the same to be advertysed that we have Receyved your letters in the behalf of Thomas Burbanck who as we knowe as well by matter of Recorde as Otherwyse to be an Evell manne so ar we perswaded that he hath maid informacion to your honor of untruethes agenst the proceedynges of our late maior Mr Kyme and others the Justices of the same Corporacion, Wherfor with no favor, and all thoughe we have just cause to deteyne hym to auswer unto severall causes (wherof here inclosed we have sent to your honor a just note, And for whome for your honors sake we have taken some pane to end the cause betweene hym and Mr Smyth) Neverthelesse because he ys come unto us with your honors letters, we have therefore thought good to permytt hym to Returne to your honor withoute ennye truble, apon your honors consideracion of the causes yow will not onely suspend your Judgement of ennye parcyall or pryvate dealing in ennye cause ayenst hym, but allso for Justice sake to send hym agen emonges us to stand to his tryall of Right or Wrong for his causes according to Equytye, Whereby as yowr honor shall show yourself to be a spectacle off justice, So shall we thinck ourselves bounden to your honor for the same, not dowpting but that our proceedings therein shalbe suche, that not onely yowr honor shall have just cause to thinck well therof, but allso that thereby he shall be tawght to knowe his dewtye fyrst towardes god, then to the quene & her lawes & thyrdly towardes hym self and the comon welthe, so knoweth Iesus who preserve your Lordshypp in much honor &c from boston this xx^th^ of December your honors to commaunde

The Maior & burgesses."

20 January 1575/6 Assembly

Anthony Kyme, Alderman, and Andrew Leake of the Common Council failed to attend, though warned. fol. 162r. **940**

The following are appointed assistants to the Dikegraves for making the Sea Dike book and allotting every man his part of the Sea Dike to be mended: Simon Melsonbye, John Gawdrye, Robert Bonner, John Hiltoft, Aldermen, Richard Draper, Richard Cowper, Jeffrey [—], John Wilkynson, John Stamper, William Sisterson, Simon Turpyn, Richard Hutchenson, Mathew Freyston (all or the majority of them). **941**

"Also yt ys Agreed att this Assemblye that the maior & the Justices, shall cause the constables of this burrowe to bring before theme Att there Tyme appoynted all servantes & Labourers within this burrowe for Direccion & order to be taken for theme according to the Lawe". **942**

23 January 1575/6 Assembly

It was ordered that every boat coming down to Boston with victuals or fuel and there discharging should pay ½d for every ton or load weight. **943**

John Hiltoft, Alderman, and William Dallands of the Common Council failed to attend, though warned. **944**

2 March 1575/6

fol. 162v.
945 It was agreed to enter into a bond to John Hiltoft, gent., in £100 for the payment of £50 on 18 January next at the Guildhall.

946 Thomas Wryght's cattle are to be distrained for £10 "extreated" against him out of the Pipe Office upon the forfeiture of a recognisance.

947 The Bailiff is to warn Richard Lyethe to come to Mr Mayor to discuss the house where he dwells before the next Assembly when order shall be taken for its repair or disposal.

948 "Item yt ys to be noted that att this assemblye a matter being arysen apon certen words spoken by John Gawtrye one of the Aldermen of this Burrowe unto Mr Maior of the same Burrowe being put to qwestyon to theme of the comen counsell there these persons of the comen counsell whose names do hereafter followe viz. John fox Richard Draper William Dallande John Stamper John Wilkynson Richard Jeffrey Philypp Curtes Andrewe leake William Sisterson Cristofer Cowper Simon Turpyn John Harcastell & Richard Josse dyd adjuge the words afforesaid to be unkynde words, & lykewise Richard Brigges & Simon Melsonby aldermen have adjudged theme to be unkynde words, and Anthonye Clamond Thomas Doughtye George Earle & Thomas Owersby have lykewyse adjudged the same unkynde wherapon his fyne by the comon counsell ys assessed to xx^{s} to thuse of the corporacon".

26 March 1576 Assembly

fol. 163r.
949 Deeds sealed: a lease for 21 years to Laurence Clark for two tenements, a piece of pasture, and a piece of waste ground impaled on the west side of the water, at a yearly rent of 17d for the tenements and pasture, and 20d for the waste ground; a lease for 21 years (dated 16 August 1575) to William Closse for three tenements (part of the Erection Lands) on the west side of the water, at a yearly rent of 21s; another lease to William Closse for 20 years of a piece of pasture called the "harp" on the west side of the water, and a little garthing stede under 3 tenements of the corporation, at a yearly rent of 12s; a lease
fol. 163v. for 21 years (dated 12 March 1575/6) to Richard Feilde, Mayor, of a cottage in the Forde End on the west side of the water sometime in the tenure of Thomas Burton, shoemaker, (part of the lands given for finding a bedesman and others in the church of Boston) at a yearly rent of 13s 4d; a deed poll for one rood of pasture in Wormgate sold to Simon Turpyn 16 Eliz.; the charter for the incorporation of the glovers dated 16 March 1575/6; a deed poll (dated 16 March 1575/6) touching a release made by Simon Melsonbye to the corporation of

the manor of Roos hall in Boston, Skirbeck and Wiberton, and a letter of attorney to Richard Turner, Serjeant at Mace, to take livery of seisin; and a deed poll sealed by Richard Bonner, Alderman, of a messuage in Wormgate where Widow Couche used to live, and a letter of attorney to Richard Turpyn to take livery for the corporation.

25 March 1576

William Gannocke, George Erle, and John Hiltoft, Aldermen, were put in election for the mayoralty and George Erle was chosen Mayor. fol. 164r. **950**

"At thys Daye yt was ordered & decreed by Mr Maior thaldermen & comon counsell of this burrowe, that comon counsell of the same shall yerelye attend & accompanye Mr Maior & thaldermen of this burrowe apon our ladys Day in the hie qwere att the Service tyme after the Eleccon of the Newe maior, And in lykemanner of maday After the newe Maior hath taken his othe for the maioraltye Afforesaid". **951**

INDEX OF PERSONS AND PLACES

References in Roman figures relate to the introduction; Arabic numerals are used for the text. Lincolnshire places are quoted without further description; most other places are defined by county.

INDEX OF SUBJECTS